ADVANCE PRAISE FOR
WHERE IS MY RED DRESS?

"There are times in your life when the words of another person stimulate, influence, inspire and instruct you in ways that profoundly move you from one emotional state to another. Sometimes this is when you inadvertently stumble across a video or when you find yourself in a room with someone you barely know, but once encountered, touches you deeply in an intimate, primal way. All of this and more is the effect of the beautifully written and provocatively felt *Where Is My Red Dress?* by Rev. Dr. Rita Andriello-Feren. In this daringly awesome account of Rev. Dr. Rita's journey through insecurity, self-doubt, abusive relationships and, in the end, a transcendent understanding of who and what she is, Rev. Dr. Rita brings the reader to a personal understanding of their own life. In doing so, she reminds us all of the "Red Dresses" we have perhaps ignored for far too long. It's time for us to give that dress another look.Thank you for that, dear Rita!

~Rev. Dr. James Mellon, Author, *The Five Questions*

Where Is My Red Dress? is a transformative journey of Rita's quest for authenticity and self-love. With honesty and vulnerability, she peels back the layers of doubt, family expectations, and fear to reveal the bold, empowered self that she has always been. Rita's journey reminds us all that the power to live authentically lies within us, waiting to be embraced. Her storywill inspire you to look within and find your own version of the "red dress"—your truest, most vibrant self."

~Beverly Eager, LCSW, Licensed Clinical Social Worker; DCSW, Diplomate of Clinical Social Work

"In *Where Is My Red Dress?*, Rita Andriello-Feren unapologetically and courageously lays bare all her secrets and demons to find her true, authentic self. While delving deep into the roots of her thoughts and attitudes about sensuality and sexuality, she discovers that both the spoken and unspoken words from her childhood had the power to chart a course filled with doubt, conflict, and a desire to please others. Growing up at the same time as Rev. Rita, I too was influenced by the expectations, morals, and music that painted a picture of how a "good girl" should act and look. It stifled the very essence of what many of us were feeling but were afraid to truly explore."

Rita takes us through her journey of marriage, motherhood, and career, all the while aware that there was still more to discover within her precious soul. She enhances her process with insights from not only spiritual and religious perspectives but also from science. By the end of the book, I wasn't just celebrating her faith in herself and her

desire to be whole—I began wondering about my own "Red Dress." An amazing read for anyone questioning and seeking to understand the journey a woman must take to find true authenticity, and the outside influences that often get in the way."
~Dana Craig Baier, Licensed Marriage & Family Counselor

"Where Is My Red Dress? by Rita Andriello-Feren is a thought-provoking, well-written, and radically truthful memoir by a wise, healthy, and whole woman. It is also a nuanced and profound inquiry into sensuality, sexuality, and spirituality in our patriarchal world. *You don't want to miss this compelling read!"*
~Debra Valentina, Soul Project Midwife, Published Author, & Writing Coach

"Rita Andriello-Feren shares her personal story with vulnerability and rawness, while interweaving metaphysical insights to offer deeper meaning. She further supports her story with research on precognitive imprinting starting in the womb and the conditioning we receive from our parents, which includes all of their unprocessed emotions. While writing about how we develop unconsciously, the author brings the light of consciousness to these experiences. Rita owns that red dress of self-empowerment—and we do too. This book is a statement to all who have walked a similar path from unconsciousness to consciousness, sifting through what is real versus projection, expectation, and the roles imposed by our birth families and society. *Where Is My*

Red Dress? is a step into the authentic self! Rita has written a powerful and courageous story that resonates deeply with my own personal journey. I highly recommend this book to anyone on the path to reclaiming their authentic self."
~Isha Doellgast, Visionary Artist, Massage Therapist

"As I write this review, I proudly wear my "Red Dress," knowing that when I have it on, I am not merely standing with, but *as* the Holy Grail I seek. Dr. Rita's book is authentic and honest (or should I say, *AWEthentic* and *AWEnest*). The vulnerability with which Dr. Rita tells her story invites the reader to re-examine those aspects of life that might be buried or shrouded in shame. I am grateful for the gift of reevaluation—and I didn't even realize I needed to do that until reading *Where Is My Red Dress?* Dr. Rita's book was the perfect guide, helping me reconsider some of my past experiences and see them for their beauty. Her writing encourages the reader to break free of molds they have created themselves or that have been imposed by society. This is truly a fun, fast, and more importantly, impactful read! I can't wait to share it *and* read it again! Find your Red Dress—it's closer than you think!"
~Rev. Dr. Liza Marquez

"As I write this, I don't know where to begin. So much of this book spoke to me and stirred something deep within. At times, I found myself in tears; I felt a churning inside, as though the dust of time that had carefully lain undisturbed, covering the deepest parts of me, was being swirled and lifted away. Rita Andriello-Feren's book *Where Is My Red Dress?*

is a true gift. To be honest, it was a gift I wasn't sure I wanted to open. But through Rita's unflinching and unwavering courage in sharing her journey, I found my own courage rising.

One of my favorite go-to sayings is, "We can't change what we don't see." I can only speak for myself, but often, even when I see the things I need to, I turn away, believing I might not have what it takes to truly look and sit with the discomfort that often accompanies growth.

While reading *Where Is My Red Dress?*, I felt like Rita was holding my hand and heart, whispering, "You've got this; it is time." Our past doesn't define us unless we let it. Just because we don't look at something doesn't mean it's not there, unconsciously shaping our life experience. With Rita as your guide, be willing to shine a light of consciousness on the places you may have feared to go. It is the only path to true freedom.

I am taking my red dress out of the closet and wearing it proudly. There is more work to do, but I am willing to do it—and now I know that I don't have to do it alone. I invite you to read *Where Is My Red Dress?* and join me. I believe this is the beginning of a movement where, together, we can embrace our sensual, sexual, and spiritual wholeness and challenge the unspoken norms that have shaped women's lives for far too long!"

~Rev. Dr. Lori Savage

"Rita Andriello-Feren's latest book, *Where Is My Red Dress?*, is a deeply personal exploration of what it means to be a fully expressed, authentic woman. Her challenging path to self-acceptance is a journey that many women—and men—can relate to. Her ultimate message is one of hope: we can overcome the lessons of our childhood and blossom into who we truly are."

~Sue Buckley, Editor at Proofreading Professionals

"Rita exposes her most vulnerable feelings throughout this book. Her story, from a young age to her current age, is one of exploitation and personal growth, as she beautifully describes her search for her sexuality and her understanding of what she wants in life regarding her desires. It is quite a journey that she lays out. To me, it felt like raw emotions were exposed to help explain her experiences. I believe Rita's story can be a great guide for young women who are also searching for clarification regarding their sexuality and who have been made to feel shame in doing so. Men could also learn much about what many women go through in their search for self-discovery."

~Terry Sheehan, Friend, Past-Life Therapist

Where is my Red Dress?

One Woman's
Sensual, Sexual, Spiritual
Journey to Wholeness

Rita Andriello-Feren

010125

Cover Design: Lori Savage

Proofreader: Sue Buckley

Layout and Design: Thor Challgren

Disclaimer: The names and identifying details of some characters and events in this book have been changed to protect the privacy of the individuals and their descendants. Also, some characters might appear as composite characters representing a single person.

Also by Rita Andriello-Feren

This Thing Called Treatment:
The Origin of Spiritual Mind Treatment

What Do I Need to Know?
101 Thoughts That Changed My Life

Please visit Amazon.com

Contents

Dedication

This book is dedicated to the child within all of us that longs for wholeness, that longs to remember that being spiritual includes all of life's riches.

Foreword

W hat an honor it is to write the foreword to this powerful manuscript, *Where Is My Red Dress?*, written by Rita Andriello-Feren. I take a long pause before allowing myself to express the profound reaction I had to Rita's courageous, daring, loving, vulnerable, transparent, and life-changing book. You see, this is not just any other book or any other author to me. I have always known what a great writer Rita is because I have witnessed the magic she brings to the written word through her talent as a storyteller and wordsmith. This incredible lady is not only my colleague, co-spiritual director, and the founder of CSL Kaua'i and the Institute of Magnificence, but for 25 years, she has also been my partner, my wife, and my best friend.

This is a book that I believe will spark a movement for all women who dare to claim their power, sensuality, sexuality, and pure spirituality as one. The phoenix of a woman's truth is rising with this life-changing manuscript, and it will never return to the ashes of secrecy and shame.

Without giving away any surprises, I want to speak for a moment about the incredible courage and love Rita shows her inner child through this book. As an inner-child advocate, I have included the inner child's wisdom in all my work as a spiritual counselor, teacher, and facilitator. What I have found in my work is that inner children do not need to understand the events of growing up as much as they need to reveal their feelings and emotional connections to those experiences. As you will read, Rita meets her feelings and emotions and gives her little girl permission to have a voice and claim her true identity. With complete transparency, Rita boldly offers us the key to freeing our own inner child. Her story provides a safe space for that part of ourselves to grow up and claim our true selves. No longer hiding, Rita proudly wears her red dress and embraces all the feelings and emotions that come with it. I can already hear inner children, both male and female, applauding Rita for freeing them from the darkness of secrecy and shining the light of truth on all their experiences.

Where Is My Red Dress? is a treasure chest of golden nuggets for each of us. Rita's intention is not to shock us but to educate us on our potential for wholeness. She does not glorify the events or victimhood. In fact, she makes it clear that each of us has a red dress that is uniquely ours. She challenges us to wear that red dress with pride, despite societal, family, or even our own self-imposed judgments.

If a man is fortunate enough to find this book in his hands, he might just become a better man after reading it. I know I am transformed and filled with a deeper understanding of what it means to be a woman after reading *Where Is My Red Dress?* I feel educated about what women have experienced and endured simply because of their gender. I am also enlightened about how history has portrayed women and the roles they've been given by men and society.

There is another gift I received from this book that I would like to share. I was not surprised or shocked by the events Rita shares because I know so much about her. As you will soon find out, I was actually a part of her story. The gift was that this book allowed me to get to know this talented, gifted, courageous, and loving person in a whole new light. I have a brand-new love affair with her. I am surprised at myself because I did not think I could love her more than I already did.

Congratulations to Dr. Rita Andriello-Feren on this daring adventure that she shares with the world. What an honor it is to know you and to share my life with you.

Dr. Patrick Feren
Spiritual Director, CSL Kaua'i, Author, and Husband

Introduction

*I hate society's notion that there is something
wrong with sex. Something wrong with a woman
who loves sex.*

~Alessandra Torre, author

I remember growing up on Long Island, New York in the
1950s and 1960s. With everything going on in the world
at the time including the position of women as homemakers
and their less-than-equal status to men in the workforce,
coupled with being born into a patriarchal household, I
came away with many confusing thoughts about sexuality,
sensuality, and how I was supposed to express myself as a
woman. I will say that I have overcome much of the confusion and shame regarding my sexual feelings and sensuality,
yet I can still feel the pull to place a false veneer between my
natural sensual self and how a woman is supposed to present
herself in the world. Compounding the issues of sexual and
sensual identities is my life as a Spiritual Director of a church
organization.

Metaphorically speaking, my sensual journey reminds me
of the Bible story of Adam and Eve when they recognized

their nakedness as something that needed to be covered up. At one time, they ran naked, free, and unafraid. As soon as their attention was drawn to it, it could no longer feel "natural." Before I go any further, I will differentiate between these two words, "sexuality" and "sensuality," as I will be using these terms throughout the book.

Gina Shaw, in her article *Sensual vs. Sexual: What's the Difference?*, on WebMD.com writes:

> Sexuality and sensuality have a lot in common—but they're not the same thing. What is the difference between being sexual and being sensual, and how do the two relate to each other? "Sexual" is straightforward: When people talk about sexual activity, they're usually referring to the process of physical intimacy between consenting persons. Sometimes, though, the idea of being "sensual" is lumped in with being sexual.

In the same article, Richard M. Siegel, PhD, a licensed mental health counselor and co-director of Modern Sex Therapy Institutes in West Palm Beach, Florida is quoted:

> I think people often use "sensual" when trying to say [or imply] "sexual-light," when it would be so much more helpful to remember that sensual simply means of the senses—sight, smell, sound, taste, and touch. In other words,

being sexual pretty much always involves being sensual—could you have sex without engaging any of your five senses? But being sensual does not have to involve being sexual. It's much bigger than that.

Gina Shaw quotes Rosara Torrisi, PhD, a certified sex therapist, founding director of The Long Island Institute of Sex Therapy, and co-host of the podcast *Our Better Half*:

> Sensuality is the basis of how we experience our bodies, other bodies, and the world around us. Sensuality is a way to positively inhabit the body, through pleasure and joy and fun and celebration. Enjoying your body can be a revolutionary act when you are not objectified or subjected to another person, and you own your pleasure and your time.

I believe we are sensual beings who may or may not decide to engage in sexual activity. But when we do, I believe understanding our sensual nature is important to a healthy and loving expression in our sexual activity.

Over the years, I have definitely let my sexuality out in ways that were not mentally and emotionally healthy for me. However, I regret little of my past. I can see that when someone receives confusing messages, or perhaps no guidance at all, about their sexual and sensual nature, she would have to create her own footsteps through the forest of that confusion. I believe I have finally come home to healthy acceptance and love for myself as a sensual, sexual, and spiritual being. I also know that there is still more here for me to uncover and heal.

My knowing for this book, through my own personal sharing, is that I can untangle the threads of confusion that block the healthy expression of sensuality and sexuality as our Divine Nature, the very Life Force of creation, not just procreation.

I am not just writing about "having sex." I am grateful for a healthy sex life, but there is more. I am writing about accepting myself fully for all my sensual feelings. I am talking about the deep knowing that the sexual life force is my Creative Spirit and the deepest part of my connection to Source Energy. The sexual life force in all of us, although sometimes misplaced, is not lessened by the way we use it. It is still here within us waiting for our recognition and joyful acceptance.

Please do not mistake my words as an excuse for promiscuity or disregard for others. The very sexual energy in all of creation is God. To be clear, I am not talking about God as some great man up in Heaven on a cloud. I am speaking of our Inner Divine Nature. Through many years of exploration and seeking, I have come to understand that each of us is a unique expression of the Divine. Mother Nature knows what I am talking about, as she is constantly giving of herself as creation, never holding back, abundantly expressing herself in all her beauty. As Leonardo Da Vinci once wrote, "Vitality and Beauty are gifts of Nature available to all who adhere to her Laws." What is more vital and beautiful than the natural expression of our sensual nature? We see it in a rose, as well as in the woman or man who feels and sits comfortably in his/her own sensuality.

Movements like "MeToo," so valid in uncovering the terrible violations made against both men and women, leave many of those violated still victimized. For those not familiar with the MeToo Movement:

> The MeToo movement is the awareness movement around the issue of sexual harassment and sexual abuse of women in the workplace that grew to prominence in 2017 in response to news reports of sexual abuse by American film producer Harvey Weinstein. While the phrase had been in the lexicon for more than a decade, a tweet by American actress Alyssa Milano sparked a social media phenomenon that raised awareness, gave voice to survivors, and led to sweeping cultural and workplace changes. The movement is credited with giving visibility to the scope of violence within the United States and across the world. It is also defined by a push for accountability, including examining power structures in the workplace that had enabled misconduct, and, in some cases, renewed efforts to seek justice for survivors through criminal and civil court systems. In the first year of the movement, numerous prominent men lost their jobs after they were publicly accused of wrongdoing. ~http://tiny.cc/bnxwzz

I do believe that when someone feels accepting and healthy about their sexuality and their body, they would never do anything to harm themselves or another. Integrity, true self-acceptance, and self-love are the ingredients of a healthy sexual/sensual being. The MeToo movement is proof enough that we continue to desecrate this most beautiful, creative gift. When I cannot feel free to be all of me, the sexual, the sensual, the emotional, the spiritual, the intellectual combined as one whole, when I cut off any part of me, then I am not expressing the wholeness that is my True Nature. This True Nature is what I term "My Red Dress." You will understand this metaphor more deeply as you continue to read.

In this book, I might add a little research here and there about the history of sex through the ages. Being conscious of the past and our inherited subconscious programs that promote the "being more virtuous is good" feeling within our culture can be helpful in our healing process. However, I am more interested in letting go of the programs and awakening our own intuitive powers that hold our own answers to self-healing. We can blame our past programming for only so long. Do we want to move forward? Do we want to live fully? Emotionally, sexually, spiritually, and intellectually? I trust as I share my journey with authenticity and transparency, it will be an example of transformation to assist all who read.

Please note that this book, *Where Is My Red Dress?*, should not be confused with the Red Dress Movement, which I will not address here. Should you want further information about that you can Google it.

~ http://tiny.cc/wnxwzz

My red dress is a symbol for the deep sensual and powerful part of myself and all women who long to feel free, sensual, and alive in their totality. Although this book speaks from the woman's point of view about women, I believe that if a man finds this book in his hands, it is meant to be there. He too can learn something about his own sensual/sexual self and that of the women he encounters.

This book will hopefully provide a roadmap for my own granddaughters and others of the younger generation who might have lost or have never known their True Selves, their wholeness. I trust that as I share the not so healthy experiences I had during puberty and beyond, it might be a guide for other young people to seek out strong mentors to educate them and lead them gently to adulthood. This book will also hopefully assist the mature and aging woman to know that sensuality is a lifelong gift that never ages. Whether it expresses sexually in intimate relationships, or in the expression of art or music or dance, or in a deep relationship with Mother Nature, our sensuality is an eternal gift that never stops giving of herself.

May this book be a guiding light to wholeness for all who read it.

Love and Blessings,
Rita Andriello-Feren

Part I - How Life Got To Be the Way It Is!

Furthermore, we have not even to risk the adventure alone, for the heroes of all time have gone before us. The labyrinth is thoroughly known. We have only to follow the thread of the hero path, and where we had thought to find an abomination, we shall find a god. And where we had thought to slay another, we shall slay ourselves. Where we had thought to travel outward, we will come to the center of our own existence. And where we had thought to be alone, we will be with all the world. ~Joseph Campbell, *The Power of Myth*

Chapter 1

Red: Good or Evil?

There is a shade of red for every woman.

~Audrey Hepburn

I was in my thirties and out with my mother experiencing the world of clothing consignment shops in Palm Beach, Florida. The day was all about looking for elegant clothes for a dinner party we were all attending. Palm Beach consignment shops have some very stylish clothes, barely used, because some women wouldn't wear a formal dress more than once at a public occasion. They were an affordable place to start on our journey. My father happened to tag along as the driver.

I was strolling through the store and picked what I thought was a beautiful red dress, glittering with sequins. I proceeded to the dressing room to try it on. As I looked at myself in the mirror, I was sure this was the dress. It was absolutely gorgeous and the color suited my dark skin and dark hair. I proudly walked out to show my mother and father my newly found treasure. The first words out of my father's mouth were "Ah, *puttana!*" If you do not know the meaning of the Italian word *puttana*, it translates to "whore." He said it half-jokingly, with a sarcastic sneer, but the message was clear: *No daughter of mine will wear a red dress when she is out with me.* Reverting back to my childhood, the shamed little girl in me slinked back into the dressing room to take that dress off and find something more acceptable and pleasing to the man who still had so much control over her feelings of self-worth.

The contradiction in my father's remark was that, on numerous occasions he told me how much he loved the color red. We even had a room in our house painted red. Why was it that a red dress on me brought such powerful disdain from his lips? When spoken by such an authoritative figure as my father was to me, that word and the subtext behind it was felt deeply in my psyche. His careless comment triggered the many things he had criticized me about before that day in the dress shop. I thought I'd outgrown those criticisms and was an independent woman in my thirties, but obviously I was not. The unhealed little girl in me was very present.

I'm sure if I asked my father about that day, he might barely remember it. However, for me, that quick reactive remark flamed my unhealed shame regarding my sexuality and feelings of being a "bad girl." Was I a whore? At times I might have acted like one as you will discover while reading this book.

(On a side note, I know the word whore might not be considered a politically correct term, but in this book, I'm not trying to be politically correct. I'm sworn to honesty).

As I am writing this book, I am still wondering why the color red or a red dress brings out such a powerful reaction in some people. Do you remember the movie The Matrix?

Red is a very significant color in that movie and the red dress is designated as a statement of power. In an article in Screenrant, wrote this:

What the Woman in the Red Dress Really Means

On analyzing one particular scene in The Matrix, it becomes clear that the woman in red is a deliberate distraction, a simulated character who is a part of the Agent training program. While the woman appears harmless, she wears a vibrant shade of red to distract trainees, triggering what's known as the "red dress effect"—a phenomenon where women wearing red are perceived to be more attractive and open to sexual advances than those in plain colors. This doesn't just apply to form-fitting dresses; the "red dress effect" has been shown to work even in a study where subjects were shown a photo of a woman wearing a white T-shirt and a red T-shirt in the same style. Her character also alludes to the Scarlet Woman or the Whore of Babylon, references lifted directly from the Book of Revelations...

Before this, I'd never heard of "the red dress effect." As I continued my research, I found that the red dress is associated with danger, seduction, and sex. In the Christian religion, the red dress is often seen as a symbol of sin and temptation. In contrast, in the Chinese culture, red is associated with good luck and happiness. The red dress and red are important symbols that have a wide range of meanings and associations.

The color red is associated with various elements, from blood, fire, and rage to love, passion, and courage. This color is all about extremes and forces that drive us towards our passion. Red also has a historical significance. Roman, Mayan, and Egyptian warriors usually wore red or colored their bodies in red to celebrate victory in war.

Is red good or is it evil? The answer to that question can be quite confusing. In the Catholic faith, there is a spiritual meaning behind the color red.

> Even when a cardinal is engaged in his ordinary daily business, his garments are edged with the red which has come to be associated with his dignity. A brilliant red glows from the piping and cloth-covered buttons on the everyday black cassocks, and from waist sashes, skull-caps and stockings. On ceremonial occasions, the cardinals' cassocks are entirely in red, and they wear red silken cloaks with voluminous trains which they drape over the arm like the Romans did their togas. Cardinals have continued to be associated with the color red, and within the Roman Catholic Church the color has become symbolic of a willingness to shed blood in martyrdom for the Faith.

The official reason why Catholic cardinals wear red robes is that the color signifies the blood of Christ. One might presume from this, that they wish to associate themselves with the Passion of Christ." (From Look and Learn: www.Lookandlearn.com)

So, is red a holy color or a whorey color? I remained confused and continued my research. The red dress is a powerful symbol with a long history. In the western world, it has been associated with passion, danger, and excitement. For centuries, it has been seen as a color of femininity and power. There is red symbolism everywhere we look. Think about it: red traffic lights signify stop. Then there is the red-light district named for the prostitutes that reside there. Then what about the phrase "seeing red," which indicates that someone is angry and on the brink of doing something dangerous.

There are New Age messages about red also: "... Red is considered the densest and slowest moving vibrational wave, and that includes everything from very dark shades of red to light pinks. And being the color of the root chakra...It also represents the material world." (Sarah Regan: http://tiny.c c/9oxwzz)

I understand that red has a range of symbolic meanings throughout different cultures and religions. These symbols include: life, health, vigor, war, anger, courage, love, religious fervor, and lust, to name a few. Would you agree that all these symbols signify passion in some way?

On a scientific note, did you know that in moments of rage or embarrassment, bright red oxygenates our blood and it rushes to the skin's surface? According to the *Philosophical Transaction and Royal Society B Journal*, "There are many theories as to why human and non-human species have evolved this physiological trait; however, many center their conclusions around asserting dominance or appearing more attractive to a potential mate." A study published in the journal Nature found that several soccer teams achieved greater match results while wearing predominantly red shirts than while playing in other colors such as white and blue.

As you can see, the diverse beliefs surrounding red can make each of us wonder what we are portraying by adorning ourselves in this color. Also, as I will later discuss, these ideas, beliefs, precepts, and opinions are seeded into the Collective Consciousness and affect our individual belief systems.

I've come to the conclusion that we can all decide for ourselves whether or not we will wear red and for what reason. I am for choice, for as the mystic, author, and 20th-century spiritual leader Ernest Holmes wrote, "We cannot live a choiceless life. Every day, every moment, every second, there is a choice. If it were not so, we would not be individuals." ~*Science of Mind,* page 143

At our spiritual center here on Kaua'i, we've started celebrating "Red Sunday." At first, it was called "Red Dress Sunday" and only the women participated. I made it clear that wearing red was a choice, and if we did, we agreed that we were wearing it to signify passion, courage, strength, and sensuality. Soon the men started asking why they couldn't wear red? I was happy about this because it meant that everyone was getting into the idea that it was okay to celebrate being passionate and powerful and to freely express it in this way. Also, it was fun and a way of practicing unity.

Years later, after that day with my father in the consignment shop and after he had passed away, I wrote and performed my one-woman show, *Tomatoes on a Windowsill*. In the last scene, to affirm my independence and coming of age, I stripped down to a red dress and sang the sacred song, *Ave Maria*, in his memory. It was a rite of passage for me in that I freed myself from what I conceived as my father's label of me as a *puttana*. I could be sacred and sexy at the same time.

Here is my closing monologue from that play:

> Daddy, I'm starting all over. I am a Nonna (Grandma). But I'm a different kind of Nonna. I wear red dresses and I got married again. That man who ignited my dream ignited a few other things too... Daddy, if you really look at my life, you'll see I didn't really toss aside all you taught me. I have a great love and appreciation for art and music, an enjoyment of good food. I'm a fabulous cook. And I'm in tune with my spiritual side...I know...we didn't always see eye-to-eye on that one, but hey, God is God. I bet you know that better from where you are now than I do. I took everything I was taught, mixed it with a little of this and a little of that,

and came up with my own recipe. Kind of like
what we do with our family recipes. We add
our own touch, our own spice, our own flavor,
but never forgetting the base from which it all
came...

I believe that all of what we are taught as children does
have an effect on our psyche and how we live as adults. It is
only when we dive deep into ourselves, let these beliefs reveal
themselves to us, that we can do the inner work to reject or
embrace what we find. Not all of us are actors and writers
like me, but I chose this art form to truly move through all
of it. Have I done that? As I will continue to reveal, I'm still
working on it.

Since I believe in the eternality of my soul, I believe choice
is also an eternal gift practiced here, in our pre-earth life
and in whatever comes next. For me, I do not condemn my
parents; instead, I believe I chose my parents to learn the
lessons I needed to learn to advance my consciousness in this
lifetime.

Chapter 2

The Cobwebs in Our Subconscious!

The conscious mind may be compared to a fountain playing in the sun and falling back into the great subterranean pool of subconscious from which it rises. ~Sigmund Freud

Consciousness studies inform us that 95 percent of our brain activity is subconscious and outside of our awareness. This subconscious is not only our own subconscious mind; it is also the Universal Mind that is common to all of us. We are living in an entangled universe where everything is connected. Transcendentalist Ralph Waldo Emerson wrote, "There is one mind common to all individual men. Every man is an inlet to the same and to all of the same."

One of the first principles of quantum mechanics is the principle of inseparability.

The universe appears fundamentally inseparable. The universe appears to be a thoroughly interconnected interpenetrating whole. Inseparability implies that we are an integral part of everything and everyone.

~Mel Schwartz, The Possibility Principle

Ernest Holmes, Founder of the Science of Mind, once wrote:

> Subjective Mind, being Universal, the history of the race is written in the mental atmosphere of the globe on which we live. That is, everything which has ever happened on this planet has left its imprint on the walls of time; and could we walk down their corridors and read the writings, we should be reading the race history...There is a tendency, on the part of all of us, to reproduce the accumulated subjective experiences of the human race.

If this is true, and from my research it seems to be, it would mean that even before we arrived here in these bodies, we were born into the consciousness that preceded us. Before I awakened to this scientific truth, I spent much of my life thinking without knowing that I was thinking. I put the blame for my life on the outside and others. I didn't take responsibility for my thoughts, nor did I know that I could change them. I trust that this book will allow the reader to at least think about the beliefs that might have been handed down to us, the power of our thoughts and our ability to change them.

What are some of the worldviews that have been passed to us that might be affecting our thoughts about sex and our bodies? In an article from *Bare Marriage*, I found some thoughts from the Middle Ages. You can investigate this site more if you choose as it deals with sexual beliefs and practices of the past and how they affect us. Here are some of those beliefs from the Middle Ages:

1. People believed that sexual sin brought Divine Punishment. Sexual sin was designated by the religion of that time. This falsity came about because when a man slept with many women or a prostitute, he would get diseases, known today as STDs (sexually transmitted diseases). These diseases, at times, proved fatal. People weren't educated about medicine so it is no wonder they had to look for an answer somewhere else. Why not point a finger back to themselves and what they considered their bad behavior being punished by God?

2. Sex was considered a sin that was made permissible if performed in marriage for procreation. People were expected to produce offspring so the missionary position was the only one approved because it was the best position to impregnate the woman. The reason was the "force of gravity." Any other form of sex, including oral or anal sex, was frowned upon and considered a sin.

3. It was believed that women desired sex more than

men and were prone to sexual temptation. Perhaps this came from the story of Adam and Eve and because women became more sexually "horny" when menstruating or when pregnant. Of course, it was considered a sin to have sex during those times because sex would not lead to reproduction.

4. There was definitely a double standard that favored the male. Women were to remain chaste and practice fidelity, but men often went to prostitutes because it would be more acceptable to degrade a prostitute than his chaste wife. And it was acceptable for a man to sleep with a prostitute, but not with another man's wife. That would be a sin.

5. Men were not punished for soliciting prostitutes and received very little reprimand for adultery. However, it was a more serious offense for a woman and sometimes led to stoning or death. Women were restricted from having sex on certain days of the week, feast days of saints, and during pregnancy or when menstruating or breastfeeding. Because the church accepted sex as a form of procreation, women were forced to churn out a multitude of children. Women faced severe social and legal consequences should they break the rules of society or the church.

I raise these points because I know how powerful the subconscious is. Is it possible that some of our feelings of shame and sin regarding our sexual expression might have been transmitted to us through the history of our species? I do believe it is. There is scientific proof now that we are even influenced in utero by the thoughts and emotions of our mothers. Biologist Dr. Bruce Lipton wrote this:

> We used to think that only nutrition was pro-
> vided by the mother to a developing child. The
> story was that genes control development; the
> mother just provides nutrition. We now know,
> of course, that there's more than just nutrition
> in blood. Blood contains information about
> emotions, regulatory hormones, and growth
> factors that control the mother's life and the
> world in which she lives. All this information
> passes into the placenta along with nutrition. If
> the mother is happy, the fetus is happy because
> the same chemistry of emotions that affects the
> mother's system crosses into the fetus. If the
> mother is scared or stressed, the same stress
> hormones cross and adjust the fetus. What
> we're recognizing is that, through a concept
> called epigenetics, the environmental informa-
> tion is used to select and modify the genetic
> program of the fetus so it will conform to the
> environment in which it's going to grow, thus
> enhancing the survival of the child. If parents
> are totally unaware, this creates a great prob-
> lem—they don't know that their attitudes and

responses to their experiences are being passed
on to their child.
~Bruce Lipton newsletter, November 21, 2014

This is not an excuse for our behavior nor does it make
us victims. There is more to this thing called "mind" than
we currently know. We are just beginning to understand
how powerful the mind is and how entangled we are in the
Unified Field. This field is energy and is invisible, so it is hard
for some of us to accept that it exists. For some of us, we are
still stuck in the Newtonian worldview that says that we are
separate from each other and subject to a deterministic universe of cause and effect. For me, I want to learn all I can in
order to become self-empowered. Knowledge is power and
I believe that understanding the power of the subconscious
and how it affects us gives us a starting point to take that
power back and make the decision to change those thoughts
and beliefs. I have spent many years in this pursuit and I
continue to peel back the layers of my own beliefs, where
they came from, and how I can change them. As I change
these beliefs, my red dress becomes more vibrant.

Chapter 3

A Mixed-Up Girl

*And one day she discovered that she was fierce,
and strong, and full of fire, and that not even
she could hold herself back, because her passion
burned brighter than her fears.*

~Mark Anthony

Let me step back into my past to give the reader a sense of the messages and metaphors I received as a child concerning my sexuality and my role as a woman. I believe our upbringing plays a major part in how we face the world and how our subconscious is developed. To support my journey, here is some research on our brain from Amanda Lee Brady, Hypnotherapist, Master NLP, and EFT Practitioner.

> **DELTA:** Between birth and two years old, the human brain functions primarily in the lowest brain-wave cycle, which is 0.5 to 4 cycles per second. These are called Delta waves. ... At this level, there is very little critical thinking or judgment taking place. ... Also, while still in the womb, your baby is receiving its programming

in this state. How a newborn baby knows how to copy your features when you smile, which is crucial in building rapport with its caregivers to aid in its survival outside, comes from a program downloaded while in this state.

From Little Rita: There was a sense of fear surrounding coming into the world. Mommy and Daddy fought a lot. I'm not sure what about. Mommy was happy to have me. She loved children and now she would have me. She spent a lot of time holding me. When I was 1 year old, Nonna came to live with us. This changed everything. Mommy's attention was centered around not just taking care of me, but also taking care of Nonna. I remember Mommy had a serious look on her face all the time. I wonder if this is why I am often told I need to smile more. Was I copying her look? Why was everyone so serious? I really do not know.

THETA: These wave frequencies measure 4 to 8 cycles per second and are predominant in children aged between two and six. Children operating in Theta are very connected to their internal world. They live in the realm of imagination, daydreaming, and still cannot show signs of critical, rational thinking. This is a super learning state, where the child is open to suggestion. These children are likely to accept what you tell them as true.

From Little Rita: *I had a lot of responsibility, especially after my brother Greg was born. He wasn't very nice to me. Was I jealous of him? I might have been. He was the boy my father always wanted. Nonna was often left as our babysitter but she wasn't very good at it. One time, I got caught under the crib when Greg somehow pushed the gate down. I was trapped and he got out of the crib. When my parents came home, I got blamed for the whole thing. It seemed that Daddy was always angry at me. I must have been a bad girl, because that is what he always said. I worried a lot too. When I went to kindergarten, my teacher called me the "worry wart." What was I so worried about? My bedroom was right next to my parent's room. I heard them fighting a lot.*

ALPHA: Between ages five to eight, the brain waves have changed into an Alpha frequency, eight to thirteen cycles per second. This is the point at which the analytical mind begins to form. Children start to interpret and draw conclusions from their environment. Still, the inner world of imagination tends to be as real as the outer world of reality. Children in this age group tend to have a foot in both worlds, using both left and right brain hemispheres at the same time. This is a great state to be in when brainstorming, creating ideas, or learning. (Schools should take note: kids learn when they are relaxed and having fun, not when they are stressed).

From Little Rita: I remember Daddy getting really sick. Mom said he had a heart attack and almost died. His friend, Uncle Filippo, told me and Greg that it was our fault. We should be better children. He told us we had better be careful or Daddy might die. I was grateful for my Grandma Hertz and my Aunt Lucile. They always told me I was good. They gave me lots of special times, like when I saw my first musical with Aunt Lucile— My Fair Lady. *I knew all the words to the songs and tried to sing along. The audience members weren't too happy about that. I found a lot of happy times with my Barbie dolls. I didn't have a Ken. I don't know why. I used my imagination and used my crayons as the other dolls. It worked. I got another baby brother, Paul. When my sister Maria was born, I was eight and I felt left out. Daddy seemed to really like her because she was pretty with blue eyes and blond hair. I do remember being jealous of her.*

BETA: From ages eight to twelve - This is the world of conscious, analytical thinking. The mind is awake, focused, and alert and is capable of logical thinking. Adults spend most of their time in this cycle.

*From **Little Rita:** Why wouldn't Daddy ever let me play? It seemed that whenever I went out to find my friends and play, I was called back home to work. I just wanted to play. Maybe Daddy would love me more for working with him on things like building stone pathways and finishing off the basement. I don't know. I don't remember a lot, but I was always scared I'd get in trouble.*

Learning about the development of the brain has surely helped me to understand my own evolution as a child and beyond. I only wish I had known all of this before bringing up my own children. However, the good news is that my determination not to repeat my past with my own children weighed heavily on their psychological and emotional development, but in a good way. I was so grateful to hear this from them, and still, I wish I'd known more. So here's how it all began for me.

In 1953, right after what was considered one of the worst times in the world, World War II and the slaughter of six million Jews, I was born to an Italian immigrant father and

a mother who I would later find out was of Jewish descent.
My mother used to tell me I was born in the middle of the
East River. In a sense, that was true, because I was born on
the island of Manhattan in New York on March 12, 1953,
eight months after my parents were married. They never told
me why I was born only eight months after they were married instead of nine months. It wasn't something we talked
about. This code of silence about sex repeats itself many
times, not just throughout my childhood, but throughout
the childhoods of many people I know. My parents never
told me I was premature; in fact, I weighed a healthy 7 lbs.,
6 oz. However, I had a hint about my parents' premarital
sex while watching their honeymoon movie. My mom was
always holding her tummy and signaling that she was nau-
seous. It was never discussed and I never asked.

Later, when my mother was close to her death, she told me
that she loved my father so much that when he kissed her, out
I came! She still couldn't talk about it at age eighty-seven. I
wonder if I didn't think asking was important enough or if I
still felt a bit awkward questioning my parents' sex life. Why
is that, and is it true for everyone? I hope this book will reveal
some of the differences between how we all talked or didn't
talk about sex with our parents. I remember the reaction
that many children have when parents broach the subject of
their sex life. "TMI! TMI! (Too Much Information), Mom,
Dad!" they scream. One of my daughters recently told me
that she felt nurtured in learning about her sexuality from
my husband and me. I like to believe that is true but I wish
I'd known more and given more information to my children.

I must be honest. There is a part of me that misses those conversations with my mother that could have happened. I would never have spoken to my father about sex, but I wish I had talked to my mom. The taboo of asking my parents about the mystery of sex might have cleared up many of my misconceptions and aided in my own sexual journey. Ah, well! Anyway, I am here, and no matter how I got here, the miracle remains. I am here.

I think I remember my birth because I recall a big, white-tiled, cold room with a bunch of people standing around dressed in white. The word I would use for the setting is "harsh." In regards to my birth, no one ever talked about it or whether they were happy I was here. I do wonder if my father wanted a boy. First-born males are important in Italian families. My father never said he'd wished I'd been a boy, but I do wonder. Do I really care if my father wanted a boy? I don't remember it troubling me or making me wish I'd been a boy. The fact that I might have disappointed him by being born a girl does not help me accept myself. I'm still here, and I'm a girl.

I believe I chose my parents before I was born, and I had a choice as to whether to be a boy or a girl. I have no proof of that but it feels right. I'm glad I showed up as a girl. I actually like being a girl. It reminds me of the song, *I Enjoy Being a Girl!* from the musical *Flower Drum Song,* I listened to that song just a few days ago and realized that after the *MeToo* movement, the words of Rodgers and Hammerstein might have to be changed if Broadway were ever to produce that musical again.

I'm a girl and by me that's only great
I am proud that my silhouette is curvy
That I walk with a sweet and girlish gait
With my hips kind of snivelly and swervey

I adore being dressed in something frilly
When my date comes to get me at my place
Out I go with my Joe or John or Billy
Like a filly who is ready at the race

When I have a brand new hairdo
With my eyelashes all in curl
I float as the clouds on air do
I enjoy being a girl

When men say I'm cute and funny
And my teeth aren't teeth but pearl
I just lap it up like honey
I enjoy being a girl

I flip when a fellow sends me flowers
I drool over dresses made of lace
I talk on the telephone for hours
With a pound and a half of cream upon my face

I'm strictly a female female
And my future I hope will be
In the home of a brave and free male
Who'll enjoy being a guy, having a girl like me.

I think about the innocence of those times when musicals such as this one were written. I didn't think of the significance of those words or whether I was demeaning myself in any way. It was just a given that "I enjoyed being a girl!" Now it seems the pendulum has swung so far in the other direction. In the 21st century, gender is always at the forefront of our conversations. There is confusion and misunderstanding in many of us. I think this is a good thing because we are finally questioning it all. I am grateful that sexual education and information is coming out in the open now in a way that makes it more comfortable for those seeking to find their sexual identity and claim it more openly. We are still a long way from normalizing this new sexuality but we are making strides.

I identify as heterosexual and "she/her." Even though I say I chose to be a girl before birth, sometimes I wonder if I am heterosexual by choice or by programming. I wonder how my childhood would have evolved in a more loosely defined world. I've never thought of anything besides my identity as a woman and having a desire for men only. I never thought of becoming anything besides a wife and mother. I learned that it was what I was made for. I wonder about nature vs. nurture. I know many young people that are fluid in their sexuality. Although I don't envy them, I wonder with open curiosity.

In my early life, I watched *Flower Drum Song* many times. I wanted to be that girl that boys fell for but the message from my family was that this kind of girl was definitely not me, or would it ever be. My parents did their best to keep me under lock and key. Like many parents, they more than likely feared that I might do what they did. However, my parents never let me know what they did or didn't do. There was a code of silence.

I'm grateful to say I am more open with my children, maybe too open. I don't care though. I want them to know everything about me. I never asked any questions of my parents, not just about sex, but about anything. I've been left with many unanswered questions, mysteries, and misinformation, and it is too late to find out now. Just the other day, I told my son to make sure to ask me anything he wanted to. I said, "I'll be gone someday and I don't want you to have to wonder like I'm doing right now." He didn't respond with any questions, but at least I opened the door that was closed to me so many times.

I remember pictures of my mom in her early days. She was gorgeous. I wondered why those pictures were cut in half. I later found out that my father cut her early boyfriends out of the pictures, or maybe he demanded that she did. It seems silly that a person wouldn't realize that someone had a life before they met them. I know my father did because he often bragged about singing under his girlfriends' balcony windows. Although it wasn't stated outright, the message was clear that standards are different for men and women. A woman being a virgin at marriage was demanded in the culture that my father impressed upon us, yet I know boys were encouraged to go out and be with women.

To his dismay, I disappointed my father in this area. I lost my virginity long before marriage. When I think about his reaction now, I wonder if he was more than likely disappointed in himself. I wonder if my appearance as a fully developed, healthy baby from an eight-month pregnancy gave him food for thought. Did he feel like he was being punished for his "sin?" I'll never know because of the code of sexual silence. However, being a parent myself, I also know that we sometimes blame ourselves for the troubles our children have.

I was held hostage by my father and mother and not allowed to date. My father made sure to tell me that he would let me know when I could go out with boys. In my adolescence, I wasn't even allowed to go on a sleepover at a friend's house. But children find their way to claim their freedom. I was no different. I would find my own ways to sexually express myself.

My father finally freed me suddenly when I turned seventeen. He simply stated that I better get out and meet boys because I would be married soon. It was quite a shock to have the doors opened so quickly and easily after so much restraint. In Italian families (at least mine), girls were born to be married and married young. As I said, I don't remember wanting anything else. Yes, I liked to sing and had a great voice, but my inner feeling was that getting married and having children would be my life. Even if I graduated from college, like my mom, I would still seek to be married and have children. My mom had a college degree and was teaching preschool when she met my father. Her career ended shortly after that. Women belonged in the home. From what I experienced, they seemed to accept that. I don't know if my mom was resentful. She never said anything. She just did what she did as a mother: cook, clean, and take care of us. I remember her coffee klatches with her friends. I often would join in just to listen to their conversations.

What's interesting about my early years is that I do not remember much about them. I've been asked what my earliest memory is and all I get is a feeling. I felt scared. It wasn't safe at my house to be me. My parents fought a lot. My dad yelled a lot. I felt like I was always doing something wrong. When my dad would come home from work, he would inspect the house. If there was a scratch on the wall or a dent in anything, he'd get all upset and try to find out who did it. I'd hide to escape his wrath.

My dad was an artist at heart who became a doctor under pressure from his family. His father forbade him to explore an artistic career and forcefully told him to become a doctor. My dad told me his father said this on his death bed, "Don't be a bum singer, Rocco. Become a doctor." He did just that but the artist in him never died. He turned every house we lived in into a sort of museum with artwork, gilded moldings, statues, and fountains. This was his passion and maybe the most important thing in his life outside of opera and good food. When I remember my dad, those memories are prevalent. I remember parties and people playacting and singing from the operas. However, I don't remember much about my mom. When I reminisce about those times, I see a woman standing watching me with a worried look while I swam in Long Island Sound or went out to play with my friends. She stood behind my dad even when he was not so nice to us. I assumed she was afraid to defend us. The house revolved around my father and what he wanted.

I would later find out that, like so many people that lived through the trauma of war, my father more than likely suffered from PTSD. We didn't know about that diagnosis in those days. I can only imagine that living in Italy during the frightening time of the Mussolini and Hitler regime and WWII would leave some serious scars on a person. Unfortunately, he turned those scars on us, his children.

My husband, who specializes in inner child work, always challenges me when I make excuses about my father and his behavior. He encourages me to talk to my little girl and take care of *her*, not my father. I believe it is very natural for a child to protect their parents. At least in my case, maybe it was about wanting to know that my father loved me. If I could blame his behavior on the traumas of war, maybe it took some of the blame off of me. Maybe, I wasn't really bad. It would take me many years to really work through these feelings.

I have memories of my parents almost getting divorced but I am the only one who remembers that. I recall lying on my father's chest at six or seven years old and seeing a speck of red blood on his white shirt. He held me as he told me that I had to make up my mind about who I wanted to live with—him or my mother. Really, no one in the family remembers this story but me. Did I make it up? Did I dream it? It seems significant, and it is, because it instilled in me the idea that I was responsible for so much in my young life. I mean, how does a six-year-old child decide which parent she wants to live with?

When my father had his massive heart attack when I was eight, his friend let me and my siblings know that it might have been our fault. He scolded us and warned us we better be good children from now on. These are the pressures that weigh on our subconscious and take years to release, if ever.

Recently, I had an experience during meditation. I realized that the subconscious programming of feeling I was bad was still there. I awoke from the meditation and wrote this:

> There once was a little girl who grew up in a home where the focus of conversation was on negativity and what was wrong about everyone. From the little girl's point of view looking up to those in authority, it seemed that it was the truth. And so when these words and thoughts were pointed at her, she took them in as that truth. Could she have been responsible for her father's heart attack? Could she always be doing something wrong? It seemed that way. However, in her imaginative playtime, she was the one in control—the boy in an adventure or the girl that got the boy. It didn't matter. She was in control and she created a world that was good and fun and happy. There was always a happy ending. That became her dream world, her play world, totally different from the one she lived in every day. She might have been called a dreamer but her dreams were real in those moments. It was hard to keep up the dream when the other world seemed so real, yet she persevered in dreaming in order to have

fun, to create the end of the story the way she wanted it to be until one day it became her reality. She thought about it. She wrote about it. She acted as if it were so, and then one day as she looked out at her world, she realized that she was living it.

We are open to suggestion and these formative years carve our future unconsciously until we become conscious of them. Fortunately, years later as an adult, I would tend to these matters through therapy and spirituality and meditations like the one above. We can change our subconscious programming. This is the good news!

To add to the confusion of growing up, there was also my Nonna. She was my father's mother who came to live with us when I was one. She arrived from Italy. My father's father had already passed away in 1944 in Italy. She left her son, my father's younger brother Frank, back home.

The things I remember about my Nonna are a bit hazy. She didn't speak much English, just enough to be understood. She was a peasant woman who still lived that way even in our house where my father was a doctor. Perhaps she never got over World War II because she spent a lot of time digging for leftover food in the garbage inside and outside of our house. One day she took me to the place where some construction workers were working on our house. She picked up a soda bottle and gave it to me to drink. I smelled urine when I lifted it to my lips and quickly put it down. Like my father, I think she might have also had some sort of PTSD from living in war-torn Italy under the regime of Mussolini and Hitler. No one would have spoken about PTSD in those days at my house, even if they knew what it was. Although feelings and emotions were expressed with lots of screaming and yelling at each other, they were not discussed. We just got through things without much thought.

I recall the stale smell of Nonna's bedroom. When I was scared in the middle of the night, I remember crawling into her bed. I sometimes wonder if something happened in that room but I draw a blank now. I only see those crimson walls in the dark and a faded memory of pubic hair. I have to mention it here because it is an indelible imprint in my mind with no explanation. I see scissors and pubic hair. It couldn't have been mine. I was too young. These are the images that imprinted themselves on me and gave me the message that sex and our bodies are secret, not to be discussed, and maybe even something vile to be avoided.

My parents often left me alone with Nonna and I remember taking care of her. She wasn't capable of caring for me. Once she fell by a tree and couldn't get up. Of course, I couldn't lift her. I was too little. Instead, I sat by her until my parents returned home.

There were good memories of Nonna too. She had the ability to sing through the whole libretto of an opera. She also loved *Dr. Kildare*, a popular TV show of the time. My siblings and I spent many nights sitting on the floor watching that show with her. These are the times I remember with a happy feeling. There is always good in everything and I believe a child will find it.

My mom's mom was my savior. Her name was Grandma Caroline Hertz. When my father, the nuns at school, and even my mom were letting me know how "bad" I was, Grandma Hertz always told me I was a good girl. I distinctly remember my father looking at me sternly and saying, "No one knows you like I do." The feeling was that I was very bad and that I had done something that could not be forgiven. I still don't know what I could have done that was so terrible.

Many years later when I was in my fifties studying to be a Spiritual Practitioner of Religious Science, the teacher asked us to write down one word that described how we felt about ourselves. I wrote "bad." Can you imagine? Even in my fifties, this was the first word that came to mind. I don't know why, but now because I trust the perfect unfolding of life, I truly believe that if I need to know, it will come forward at just the right time. As I write this book, I am seventy-one and still I can recall no incident or incidents that would have given me this label at such a young age. You might think, why didn't you talk to your parents about it in later years? The only answer I can give you is that the code of silence about matters of the heart or those deep conversations that some parents and children have were not possible with my parents. They would either say I didn't know what I was talking about, deny they ever said it, or just change the subject. I never sought to go deeper with them.

A lot has come up while writing this book and I have turned to my husband about this very thing. Thanks to him and his excellent inner child work, I actually had a breakthrough. When asking him about the blanks I had in memory about what I could have done to receive this "bad" title, he replied. "It's obvious. Why do you think you did something? You were just told, 'You're bad,' and you believed it. It was a lie. You were lied to."

What he said finally made total sense. It didn't mean I did something bad. No, my father was just acting from what he knew about raising a child. There was no truth in it and I didn't need to hunt for it again. I finally had a conscious knowing about this. I broke the subconscious pattern. However, I still reaffirm it to myself when the thought creeps back in. This is how we have to work with our subconscious minds. It's okay to bring things forth and really look at them. It is the only way we can heal. Socrates spoke these words of truth at his trial, "The unexamined life is not worth living." It's not worth living because we will never truly know ourselves until we explore every part of ourselves. Only then will we live our true authentic selves.

I recently read a book by Mel Schwartz called *The Possibility Principle*. He describes how in our early years when significant things are said to us like, "You're bad," we have a wave collapse in that moment. In other words, it becomes a groove in our brain that remembers that moment in detail and with feeling. After that, if we do not take care of it, we continue to look for reasons why that is true. We then continue to deepen that groove in the brain. It is not until we become conscious of it that we can make the changes in belief necessary to create a different, more empowering wave collapse. Dr. Schwartz writes:

These events need not be traumatic; they may, in fact, be subtle. Yet in those moments, our potential fades. It's as if we have taken a snapshot of ourselves, and we become frozen in time. I refer to these as confining wave collapses, in contrast to defining wave collapses. We are no longer the potential of the wave, but the finiteness of the particle. And we carry this picture of ourselves with us through our lives, allowing it to burden and limit us. We lose the authorship of our life story.

I love quantum science. It's taught me that everything is waves of potentiality until we hold the belief so strongly and with so much feeling that it becomes a particle and becomes our life. We tend to live in the memory of ourselves instead of the possibility of newness in the present moment. I encourage others to take the time to explore the feelings they have about themselves. Healing is always possible, even in the direst situations, and help is always available. Once we have the intention to heal, the way is made and support shows up. I know this is true.

I do not believe in bad people, only in mistaken choices that are made in ignorance. When I use the word "ignorance," I am talking about the ignorance of knowing who and what we are. Our ignorance denies us the truth that we are Divine individualized expressions of the one God, the one Perfection, the one Source. This is my belief system. It's called *The Science of Mind and Spirit*. Every Sunday at our Center on the island of Kaua'i, we tell ourselves and each other, "We are magnificent." We've been doing this for eleven years and still it is important. Sometimes people ask us why not choose another word other than "magnificent?" We always answer that we will continue until we truly embody our magnificence.

My other memories of my childhood are scattered in my mind. I remember one Christmas Eve when we moved to a new home. I was four years old and I was afraid Santa wouldn't find me. He did. That's when I got my Patty Play Pal, a three-foot doll. I remember friends that weren't very nice like someone I called Jeanie the Meany. I remember my Aunt Lucile, my mother's sister, visiting at Christmas and being the one who recognized me as the adult I wanted so much to be. She smelled like nicotine and perfume and she let me play with her jewelry and dress up in her clothes. She took me to my first musical, *My Fair Lady*. There were also other wonderful times with her, like standing out in the cold in New York City, waiting in line to get into Radio City Music Hall to see the Rockettes dance and the new Disney film of the year.

There was always an argument between my father, my Aunt Lucile, and my Grandma Hertz. They definitely did not get along. I would say they tolerated each other because of my mom. My grandma was especially verbal with my dad and didn't mind telling him off. I couldn't believe some of the things she would say to him, both in my defense, and at times, just to insult him. When he criticized what she was eating, Grandma called him a fat pig. Their bantering sounded downright cruel, but they seemed to think they were being funny.

These were my role models: a subservient mother, a patriarchal father, an independent aunt, and a grandmother who didn't mind speaking her mind. My father criticized them continually. He even blamed my aunt for bringing skin disorders into the home because he said she slept in too many hotel rooms. Later when I understood life a bit better, I realized that this comment had to do with sex. My aunt never married but she did have boyfriends. I loved one of her boyfriends so much, that at the age of eight, I asked him to marry me when I grew up. My aunt didn't mind and they both played along. It was innocent enough. Maybe my father was jealous of my comfortable relationships with my aunt and grandma. Who knows? To me, my Aunt Lucile and my grandma were my solace and the ones who totally accepted me and made me feel good and special. I was very much in my red dress with them.

Oh, by the way, I say my aunt never married, but I would find out much later that she had gotten married when she was very young but later found out her husband was a bigamist. Life is complicated!

I had one more role model. It was my father's sister, Aunt Dolores, whose birth name was Savarina. In a statement of what I'm sure was defiance, she changed her name. That's what my father told me. She was the "black sheep" of the family. She ran away with a thirty-year-old man when she was fifteen. She had two sons by this man but he eventually deserted her. Apparently my father and grandfather raised those two sons. For much of my early life my father didn't talk to Aunt Dolores. They were always fighting about something so I didn't see her very often. The only time she was mentioned was when he wanted to scold me, "You're just like your Aunt Dolores." What did I do that reminded him of Aunt Dolores? Whatever it was, it was "bad."

I often worked alongside my father and mother. Being the oldest put a lot of responsibility on my shoulders. In fact, I do not remember having much fun. I wanted to play and I tried to every time I got a chance, especially when my father wasn't home. As a doctor, he worked many hours. But when he was home, I was expected to work around the house with him. I would be called home from playing to come work on some project. On the plus side, I learned a good work ethic, but as an adult I've had to learn to relax and play.

As a child when I was out playing, I was always pretending. I made up plays, built forts, created magic shows, and re-enacted all the movies I had seen. I directed my friends in *The Wizard of Oz* and *Babes in Toyland* and *Robin Hood*. The interesting part is that I most often cast myself as the boy in the play. Perhaps playing the boy made me feel in charge of my own story. In those days, we were taught that men were in charge.

I remember my girlfriend and I playing *The Man from U.N.C.L.E*, which was a popular TV show of that time. Our play-acted story was so real that we actually shared a kiss. I never told anyone about that and I didn't question whether I preferred girls. I knew I loved boys. When I couldn't fall asleep at night, I made up more stories, usually love stories in which I was the lead. In these bedtime stories, I played the female lead, creating stories where some boy I had a crush on in real life loved me in my self-made fantasy. I guess I could say, I was a writer, an actress, and a director from an early age. The crushes I experienced were usually with older boys. I never had the opportunity to act on these crushes but they were a big part of my fantasy life. I was obsessed with falling in love.

How do I assess my childhood and what I learned from my parents, especially my father? Life is hard work. Life has behavioral rules. Food is important and a way to celebrate. Women belong at home, cooking, cleaning, and taking care of the family's needs. Women take care of men. I even cleaned up after my brothers by making beds and straightening their rooms. Most importantly, one must love God and be a good Catholic girl.

I hadn't really learned anything about my body or sex. That was a secret and never disclosed to me. I had athlete's foot as a young girl, and when I got my period at age eleven, my mother asked me to make sure the blood was not from my foot. She really meant it. I do wonder why it was so difficult for my mother to discuss these most important things with me. The things I did learn about sexuality were learned from their friends. In writing this book, I have found this is true for many of us. However, all of that would change when I turned fourteen.

My parents did their best to keep me constrained and away from boys. I even attended an all-girls Catholic school. What my parents didn't know was that I was finding my own way of being loved. This would prove to be my rite of passage.

Chapter 4

Where Is My Mother?

A mother's absence is like a missing puzzle piece;
it leaves a void that can never be fully filled
~Unknown

I have talked a lot about my father regarding my feelings about myself, but where was my mother and how did she affect my life? Where was she the day I picked that red dress out in the consignment shop? Yes, she was there, but did she say anything? Nothing that I can recall. To tell you the truth, I would be well into my fifties when I began to get to know my mother, and even then, I was left with a lot of questions concerning her life, her feelings, and especially her life before marrying my father. Where did that young girl go who sat sensually upon the beach in that picture? Who were the missing figures in so many of the photos of my mom? These are questions that will never get answered because I never asked them. I encourage us all to ask questions of our parents, even the difficult ones.

In a nutshell, from my perspective my mother was a very contradictory person. She was very religious, and yet she wouldn't mind sharing an off-color joke here and there. One of her craziest jokes in my recollection was her telling my Mormon friends that she was an "Italian by ejaculation." She said it without embarrassment. I was mortified. My mother talked about sex but only in a humorous way. It was all jokes and innuendos.

My mother was born into Judaism but this was not discussed in our family. Perhaps because it was too close to the Holocaust. I would later find out that while I always thought I was 50 percent Italian and 50 percent Jewish, I am actually 71 percent Jewish. Thank you Ancestry.com! I've never truly investigated my Jewish heritage besides acknowledging that I did have ancestors that met their death during the Holocaust. My Aunt Lucile kept these tidbits of history alive for us but only in a minimal way. I have newspaper clippings of Jewish relatives in Boston but I have never been interested enough to pursue my genealogy.

My mother never spoke of being Jewish. I don't know if she practiced it as a child. My father told me that my Grandma Hertz thanked him when he married my mother. She said, "Finally, we will put an end to all this." She was referring to the fear she felt about the Holocaust. Remember, it was only 1952 when they were married. World War II and the persecution and killing of six million Jews was fresh on everyone's mind.

When talking about her childhood, my mother mentions that she was always attracted to St. Clare of Assisi. Catholicism was my mother's religion of choice and she made sure we all knew this through her actions and her service to the church. I joked in my one-woman show that if my mother hadn't liked sex so much, she would have been a nun. My sister and I often joke with each other that it was my mother or the Hertz blood that made us like sex so much. These jokes all stemmed from my mother's comments about sex made in jest with a gleam in her eye.

My mother was a contradiction. I can't tell you what she really believed about most things but I did know that she loved Catholicism. She was secretive about everything else and hid behind her humorous nature. Later when I left home and was raising my own children, I never got a real letter from my mother. She communicated through newspaper clippings which were usually about her religion, a concert she'd seen, or some political issue. These clippings were to let me know what she thought I should be doing. She would scribble notes in the columns saying, "Did you know this?" or "Have you tried this?" or "Does your church do this?"

I know my mother truly loved Jesus and that she wanted us to love him as much as she did. She was responsible for taking us to church. In fact, if it weren't for her, we probably wouldn't have been brought up in Catholicism. My father didn't go to church nor did he practice until the last fifteen years of his life. My mother didn't drive so we walked to church. We were known as the walking Andriello Family. If we were offered a ride, the answer was usually "no." My mother thought it was good to walk and we did, even in the snow and rain.

When I ask the question, "Where was my mother?" I am asking where was she in regards to emotionally caring for me. I know we were always fed and clothed but I don't remember much else. She was aloof. I remember being sick at home and missing school but I don't recall where she was. On those sick days I spent a lot of time up in my room with a TV. Did she bring me soup? I don't remember. Although she was a stay-at-home mom, I don't know what she did other than cooking, cleaning, and catering to my father. I know that was a lot and I thank her for it but it didn't help me to get to know her.

I am a very loving person but there is a part of me that is held in secret. Did I learn this from my mother? I would say that I do not let people in easily. I have a few very close friends. Over the years, I have grown to be more open. I have worked on learning to trust, especially to trust myself to be discerning in my relationships with others. I am more open now but I remain guarded—a behavior I witnessed from my mother. I do know that once we open to who we truly are, we are not afraid to be open and honest. This is the path I am on now.

One thing that always bothered me about my mother was her dress attire. She was married to a doctor but her clothes seemed old-fashioned and not very attractive. She wore loose stretch pants, modest dresses, and baggie shirts most of the time. She was the one who held the purse strings in our family. My father must have driven her crazy because he loved to spend money on food, parties, and whatever he wanted. My memory of Christmas with my mother was her waiting until Christmas Eve to buy our tree so she could get it at the best price.

There are many instances of my mother's aloofness and covert ways of dealing with me as I was growing up. I was much older than my siblings—four to eight years older. I took a lot of the responsibility for teaching and caring for them. I was almost a mother figure to them. Later in life a friend of mine observed, "You are like their mother." At the time of that comment, my siblings were in their thirties!

Growing up, I disciplined my brothers and sister. Even with my limited understanding of it, I remember teaching my brothers about sex. When one of my brothers had his first wet dream, I was the one who explained it to him, as silence regarding sex was practiced in our home. This is why I say my mother was a contradiction. Dirty jokes were fine, but talking honestly about sex was off the table. As I write this, I can see how the confusion and lack of clarity about sex and growing up can most definitely influence us, and not necessarily in a good way. We learn on our own. At least that is what I did.

Before her death, my mother and I became closer. I am grateful for the conversations we had, even though for the most part, they were superficial. However, there was a depth to our conversations that was unspoken. I understood her and was more like her than I would admit. The deep part of our relationship began after my father died and she re-married. I would have to say that this man was the opposite of my father. He was fun and down to earth. He shared her spiritual nature with her. I was happy for my mom. I feel that she finally received back that part of herself that she might have lost with my father. She found her red dress! I saw her laugh, dance, and really have a good time. Thank you for that, Bob!

One day right before she died, my mother told me the truth. It was the last time I saw her. Her second husband, Bob, had passed away and I know she was trying to decide whether she wanted to continue to live. People can die from broken hearts. First, she told me that she loved my father very much, but that there was something even more special about her relationship with Bob. He was truly the love of her life. *Wow!* I thought. We had more in common than I realized. My second husband, Patrick, is most definitely the love of my life.

In that last conversation, my mother asked me if I remembered the story of the two swans who loved each other so much that when one died, the other decided to follow. She said she was trying to decide which swan she was—the one who wanted to live or the one who was more at peace with death. My mother most definitely made her decision. She died from cancer four months after Bob passed. It was sudden. No one knew she was so sick. Perhaps she was so busy taking care of Bob that she didn't take care of herself. This would have been like her. Bob died on Christmas and my mother died on the eve of Easter Sunday. What perfect holidays for this spiritual couple.

When people ask me if we can choose when we die, I answer yes. My mother was a perfect example of this. She chose what swan she was and everything else followed from there. We can find our red dress at any time in life and it is never too late. My mother was proof of that.

Chapter 5

Finding Love in All the Right Places?

Words can be worrisome, people complex, motives and manners unclear, grant her the wisdom to choose her path right, free from unkindness and fear.

~Neil Gaiman

At fourteen I went through my sexual rite of passage with an older man. He is gone from this earth and I hold no animosity toward him. I do believe that it strongly affected me in a sexual and emotional sense, both for the better and for the worse. However, in this moment, I've convinced myself that I am better off for having had this experience as I can never know what my life would have been without it. It is who I am and what happened to me. I want to take the good from it without lessening both its positive and negative effects on my life. I've titled this chapter *Finding Love in All the Right Places?* because I am still questioning its impact on my life. My friends tell me I was sexually abused. It wasn't normal for a girl my age to be with a man three decades older than she was, yet it seemed very normal at the time. In fact, it wasn't until the last few years that I have thought about it in any other way but positively.

He was in his early forties. I was fourteen. I will not disclose any other details about him so as not to disclose his identity. I want to be able to talk freely about this because I believe it had a major impact on my sexuality. I also believe it could help others that might find themselves in my situation.

Many years later, right before my father died, he asked me out of the blue if this man had ever touched me. I was forty years old at the time and I lied. Why should I tell him now? I never did anything against my will. The man had long since passed away and why start something that I knew would probably have ended up being held against me—another reason for me to be labeled "bad." I don't think my father believed me when I answered that question with a no but he never pursued it any further. Remember, there was that sexual code of silence in our family. I wonder if he was afraid to know the truth. I'll never know. What I can know is how this experience impacted me by finally examining it with adult eyes.

I call my relationship with this older man an affair because he was married. Is it possible for a fourteen, fifteen, and sixteen-year-old girl to have an affair? When I was in my early twenties and I became a Mormon, I confessed this relationship to one of the elders. He told me I was guiltless because the man was married and I wasn't. The Mormon elder didn't question me about anything else. I find this an interesting way to diagnose a relationship but I was relieved to remain guiltless. My affair with this man lasted three years. However, the friendship that followed lasted over thirty years. Because of the length of my relationship with him, well past the physical part, I must regard it as more than just a meaningless affair in my life. I believe it was deeper than that.

Without going into too many details, I will say that it was both the happiest and saddest time in my life. This person shared my love for nature and we shared many experiences of being in the lush and magical places on Long Island. We frequented the woods, streams, beaches, and the wilderness of New York, not to have sex, but to simply have fun. Even in his absence, I remember many days alone in the woods, lying in the snow, looking up at a blue sky that had so much meaning for me. The mystery of nature that I both felt and didn't understand poured down on me from that azure sky. I was in my "red dress," although I wouldn't have called it that at the time. It simply felt beautiful, expansive... and I felt beautiful and expansive. The earth, the sun, the moon, and the stars were my playmates and I was wholly connected to that playful part of myself. I was naturally those things but now I had someone with whom to share it.

When I turned sixteen, he wrote me a poem. For all these years, I've kept that poem and the card that went with it.

Sixteen! Is a flower awakening to spring...
A gleaming drop of dew in the morning sun...
A cluster of violets in the woods...
A patch of daisies in the fields...
A sparkling stream running through the meadows...
Sixteen is the soft rain on the forest moss...
The whispering wind through the pine needles...

A dream among the stars through a bedroom window...
Sixteen is a girl laughing and crying, singing and dancing, in
love with life and happy to be alive...
As sixteen is the spring of life...

That was me, in essence, and he noticed it. We sang together many times and he definitely loved my voice. He invited me to sing, not only the songs he liked as my father had demanded of me, but he also wanted to hear the songs that brought me joy.

Sex was definitely a part of this relationship. In fact, it was my introduction to sex. I'd never even kissed anyone up to this point. I'd never been touched nor had I experienced an orgasm. He didn't touch me and I never did have an orgasm with him. I gave sexual pleasure to him, but other than deep and wonderful kisses, I never received any sexual pleasure from the experience.

I suspect you might be judging him by now. This is where the word "abuse" comes to the foreground to classify this relationship. I have looked back on it many times and analyzed it extensively. I can see that this is also where I learned a behavior that would form a belief that would take me years to get over.

The belief that was born out of this experience was that to be loved, I must give sex. I do remember giving him sex willingly to experience that moment of being held and feel what I perceived as love.

I've italicized this because I want to emphasize that this is what would form me for the rest of my life until I finally healed it. As I wrote earlier, there was a wave collapse that solidified itself during that relationship and I lived with that belief for many years. I looked for it in every relationship I experienced after that. I would spend many years trying my best to be sexually attractive and sexually giving, without realizing that I was doing it in hopes of being loved. I would never feel good enough in the bedroom. If a relationship ended, I blamed it on myself. For a long time, I would measure the success of my relationships with how many times or how often someone would want to have sex with me. After psychologically and emotionally analyzing this, I came to realize how this overall feeling was a driving force in my life. It made me needy. It made me feel not good enough.

The love I received from this man that I didn't feel from my own father drove me to go back to him again and again to give sex. I called it love but it was the longing of a little girl to find some sense of self-worth. I would play this card many times in subsequent relationships before I would finally find that I was good enough and lovable just as I am. I would learn that I didn't have to prove anything to anyone. I didn't have to be sexy enough for anyone. I didn't have to be anyone but myself—sufficient, whole, and complete. I could be a woman of intelligence and sensuality at the same time, not for some acknowledgment from a man, but just because it was who I was. However, this wouldn't happen until many years later and after many trials and errors...and therapy.

As I neared my seventeenth birthday, I became more educated about sexual intercourse. I would sometimes beg him to make love to me. He used to tell me I would have to wait until I turned eighteen. I didn't understand this at the time but he said, "It will bind us too much." I could tell myself one of two things. I could tell myself that either he didn't want to get caught because if he penetrated me, there would be proof, or I could believe what he was saying. He knew this relationship wasn't going to last and he didn't want to bind me emotionally to him. A young girl of my age didn't understand what that meant but the woman now does. He actually did me a big favor but not without receiving his own pleasure. I could hate him for this, but I don't. I would be lying if I didn't say, at times, I have felt really angry. I feel that because of this relationship, I lost some of my childhood...actually, a lot of it.

As I continue to look at this experience now with my adult eyes, I am finally admitting the child abuse that I experienced. I am remembering one time when he brought his friend to meet me in a very private place and left us alone. This other person then proceeded to solicit sex from me. I ran from the room. However, I didn't run from the relationship with my older man. I never asked him why he brought his friend to me. I didn't want to know. I do believe I loved my older man as much as a teenager could understand love.

As I write this, an event is coming to mind that happened after our physical relationship had ended. I was married and at his home. I was pregnant and wearing a loose-fitting dress, just bouncing boobs and tummy all over the place. I didn't think anything of it but he made a comment that suggested that I should cover myself up. I believe this was a moment when he realized that I had grown up and was no longer available to him. Our relationship had long since ended but I do believe there was always a part of him that thought we would continue at some point. In fact, there were times in the future when he tried to engage me. However, at that point, I was so closed off that I simply jokingly brushed off his subtle advances.

I've titled this chapter *Finding Love in All the Right Places?* because the question is still there in my mind. I remember when the first person told me this was abuse. I still didn't want to believe it, even at the age of fifty. I clung to my faith in love and romance. My husband recently told me something that truly made me cry. "Don't you see. You made it beautiful. That's what you do with everything, even the profane."

Despite the well-meaning people who tell me that this was abuse, and I now do believe it was, I still hold a special place in my heart for this man. I can't speak for his behavior but I can speak for myself. Yes, I had to work through the psychological and emotional turmoil that this rite of passage caused me, but there is a part of me that believes my life would have turned out far worse and more difficult and challenging without him.

I was not notified about his death until a few months after it occurred. I was surprised he never contacted me to tell me he was sick. I'm sad about that because we were still good friends at that point. I can only surmise that he didn't want me to see him ill.

In closing this chapter of my life, something very strange happened one night. My ex-husband and I were on our twenty-fifth anniversary vacation. We spent some time in a clothing optional resort. I was naked in the hot tub, feeling very sensual and free, just splashing in the water and playing with my husband. I didn't call it that at that time but I was most definitely in my red dress, truly living in joy and freedom. There was a man sitting in the tub watching me and smiling. I had seen him a moment before on the dance floor. He was dressed in a shirt with no pants, just as I had seen my older man at times. As he smiled at me in the hot tub, I had this feeling that he was approving of the freedom I was experiencing. A chill went through my body. Later I would find out that this was the very weekend that my older man passed from this earth plane. Could it have been his spirit? Did he know what was to come? It was just a couple of weeks after this incident that I met the man who would completely shift and change my life—Patrick Feren.

Chapter 6

A Spirit in Rebellion

Well-behaved women seldom make history.
~Laurel Thatcher Ulrich

I was always the one who was wrong, bad, and never did what my father wanted. I was supposed to be an opera singer. That's what he wanted for me. This was a contradiction to me that I have yet to reconcile. In one voice, he was instilling in me that a woman's place was in the home, and in the other voice, he was urging me to leave my family and become a professional opera singer. I believe that the housewife side of me won out because it was ingrained in me at such an early impressionable age. I got married instead of going to college and becoming an opera singer.

Finally, when I was in my twenties and living in Farmington, New Mexico, raising a family, I thought I'd start to study singing. My love for theater and music had never subsided. I went on to become professionally trained as an opera singer. I had many amazing theatrical experiences in the Southwest but I never fulfilled my father's dream. I just couldn't reconcile leaving my young children and pursuing that type of career. My father never truly forgave me for this but I know I did the right thing. I did the best thing I knew how to do at the time. Would I change it knowing what I know now? No, I wouldn't. It's as simple as that.

I have a memory of the night of my sister's wedding when my father confronted me with his disappointment in how my life had turned out. At this point at age forty-one, I had raised three children, was happily married, graduated from college with my Master's degree, was a teacher in a private school, and had received some notoriety as a singer in the Southwest. He sneered at me and pointed to me in front of his friend, the General Manager of the Metropolitan Opera. "She could have been a star, but she refused." In that moment, in front of his friend, I tried to explain myself and defend the life I had chosen. "You are NOTHING!" he retorted to my litany of all I had truly accomplished. I didn't say a word back to him, made some excuse, and simply walked away. Inside, I was screaming, "I AM SOMETHING!"

After that night, my father never talked to me about my opera career again. It wasn't until after his death that my mother told me of his disappointment in how my life had turned out. She let me know that my father blamed my ex-husband for holding me back from the career he thought was my destiny. I felt sad that my father carried this empty torch to his life's end. I now realize that this diminishing torch was really for himself. He was the one who wanted an opera career. Do parents live their lives out through their children? Sometimes I believe they do.

As I have honestly looked back and analyzed my life, I call myself a "spirit in rebellion." The rebellion was against me and my misunderstanding of myself. I was looking for something without knowing what it was. I had that relationship with my older man, but at the same time, I was still falling in love with boys who didn't return my love. I ran away from home in the middle of the night at age eighteen. I figured out how to survive on my own but I didn't know what I wanted besides freedom from my father. I didn't leave because of the boyfriend I had met a year before at Kings Point Merchant Marine Academy. I left because I wanted to get away from the horrible restrictions under my father's patriarchal thumb. As I look back on it now, I can see how my early years set the stage for who I was to become as a woman. It was an unconscious thing but I spent much of my early life unconsciously trying to please the men I was with. If I could be good enough in bed, I would be loved.

I wandered through life for more than twenty-five years, experiencing motherhood, becoming a college graduate, having a few affairs, bringing my voice to professional singing quality, and experimenting with different philosophies and religions. I went from Catholicism to Mormonism to Shirley MacLaine to crystals and channelers and tarot card readers. Finally, in the year 1998, I found Religious Science which I embraced and eventually became a practitioner, a minister, a doctor of Consciousness Studies, and the Founder of a spiritual center on the island of Kaua'i with my second husband, Patrick Feren. Although we didn't meet until I was well into my forties, I consider Patrick the soulmate of my life here on planet Earth.

Patrick brought out my true self, took me out of my self-made role as a whore, and grew up with me in the true sense of the word—emotionally, spiritually, and physically.

I went through puberty with him, the loving kind. I was embraced for my intelligence and spiritual depth and given the freedom to grow consciously and by choice. I gave him the same gift. In essence, we were made for each other. A strange synchronicity brought us together. Although many people considered us crazy and unstable, I know we were, and still are, the sanest people in the world. We are capable of amazing things and we accomplish them. Now I believe we were brought together to find out how fantastic we are. We were brought together to discover how amazingly creative and unusual we are. We were brought together, not just to live happily ever after, but to learn that we are capable of changing the world one person at a time, beginning with ourselves. Our love is not just for us but a launching pad for the lives of others. A couple we once married put it this way in their vows and I concur, "Love is not about looking inward to the one you love, but from that place where you both reside in love, looking out together to the world." That perfectly describes Patrick and me.

I might have wanted a better childhood but what I went through has little power over what I am experiencing as a child in my seventies. I believe there are no mistakes in one's life. As Steve Jobs said:

> You can't connect the dots looking forward; you can only connect them looking back-wards. So, you have to trust that the dots will somehow connect in your future. You have to trust in something—your gut, destiny, life,

karma, whatever. This approach has never let me down, and it has made all the difference in my life.

Chapter 7

The Rite of Sexual Passage

It's not about being perfect. It's not about where you get yourself in the end. There's power in allowing yourself to be known and heard, in owning your unique story, in using your authentic voice.

~Michelle Obama, Becoming

B efore I move on to my life with Patrick, I feel it is necessary to be more clear about some of the things I spoke of in the previous chapters. I think it is necessary for you to understand where I came from in regards to men. Since I called myself a whore, which shocks but doesn't surprise me, I think I have some explaining to do.

The loves of my life have always been theater and writing. As I said, I play-acted from an early age. Love stories were my genre. I'm not sure if this is common for all little girls, but for me, I think it all stemmed from the love that I never felt I received from my father. I say, "felt I never received," because I'm sure If you asked my father, he'd say he loved me very much. I do not remember a hug from him or ever sitting on his lap, even though I once saw a picture of myself on his lap.

I do remember being taught to behave and to play the piano to accompany him as he sang. I learned about antiques and art at the age of eight on our walks on Second Avenue in New York City. When he perused old dusty antique shops, I witnessed a peace and joy within him. I was the only one of his children that accompanied him on these trips. I still wonder what he saw in me that perhaps he didn't see in my siblings. I didn't know it at the time, but I do believe he saw the artist he wished for me to become. Before he died, I recognized and accepted his love. I came to understand that the way he was with me was the only way he knew how to show me love.

At other times, I was terrified of my father because of his explosive personality. It was quite a contradiction. I do not remember many days when I did not feel afraid. Is it surprising that at age fourteen I would find myself with a father figure who made me feel my self-worth, who made me feel important, who was fun, who listened to me, and who gave me some of the most loving moments in my childhood? I never ever felt like I was doing anything wrong. It felt natural to be sexual, even though I never had a sexual feeling. I was the servant to his pleasure. I learned at an early age to rely on my sexuality in exchange for self-worth. I can truly see how this idea led me through my teens, twenties, and thirties. I say I loved men but what I really meant is that men, when I pleased them, loved me, or so I thought.

My affair with my older man ended abruptly after my father told me I could finally go out and meet some boys.

I was seventeen. I don't know what made him decide that it was time for me to date. Maybe my mother prodded him or maybe he was pushing me toward marriage. No matter the reason, I was ecstatic to be set free. I attended an all-girls school, so of course I wasn't going to find boys there. I don't recall how I ended up at the Kings Point Merchant Marine Academy outside of Great Neck, New York. The day after I turned seventeen, destiny led me there. My high school girlfriends and I attended what was called a mixer. It was my first night out and this is where I met the man, David, who would become my first husband and shape the next three decades of my life.

One month into our relationship, he and I planned our first sexual encounter. When I say "planned," I mean we sat down in a library and looked at the pros and cons of being sexual with each other. Since I truly didn't understand sex or what a commitment like this implied, I was naïve in my approach. I was attracted to him, thought I was in love, and it just seemed like the next natural step. By that point, I had never had an orgasm. I really didn't know what to expect. I don't remember ever being aroused by being kissed. Really, to put it blatantly, I knew nothing about sex. It was simply the next step when you thought you loved someone. I remember David telling me his twin sister told him to be careful before he decided to take my virginity. At the time I thought she was just trying to keep us apart, but now I see the wisdom in her words. If I have any "should haves," and I have plenty, I should have been more thoughtful or careful or known myself better before indulging in sex. However, for most of us, I surmise it is a trial by error thing. Eventually, we learn or we get burned. I had no one to ask or talk to besides my girlfriends. They were all having sex too. It was just the next natural thing to do if you thought you loved someone. Have I said that too many times?

My older man had warned me that sex would bind me to him but I had no idea what that meant until I indulged in its pleasures. How I long for it to be different for the next generation. It might be that I am ignorant of the kind of sex education that goes on in homes today, or maybe we are just meant to figure it out by ourselves. Could it be that this is the journey of our individual evolution? What I want for all of us is to not lose our deeply rooted sensuality that is our Divine nature. I wish for everyone to stay attuned to that sexual force that is the very ground of all creation and not have it clouded up in taboos, religious rules, and misunderstandings rooted in our various unconscious rites of passage. Maybe that's why I once wrote a screenplay about a woman from Polynesia who took boys through a rite of passage by teaching them about themselves through deep emotional and spiritual intimacy before the sexual act ever took place. I know there are some cultures that do just that. I am looking for an answer to the dark trials that many of us go through to find ourselves.

David and I had nowhere to go to have sex except to lay down in a secluded spot in a park. I don't remember it feeling good. I was a virgin and it was painful. What I do remember is it felt good to be loved. Being loved and sex went together for me. After that night in the park, sex was the basis of our relationship. We couldn't get enough of it. Our sexual rendezvouses took place anywhere that we could find privacy—the back of a car, under the pier on the beach, in a garage he rented to store his motorcycle, and then, of all the craziest places, in the Kings Point Machine Shop. On those nights, I had to parade with him past the other cadets who also took their girls to that little room to have sex. The cadets had it all decorated with lovely bed coverings, flowers, and candles. David and I had lots of sex. I called it love and I'm sure at the time it was. However, as I look back at it, I can see I was just a young girl, uneducated in the ways of love and intimacy. I was unconsciously living as I pleased, strong-willed, and seemingly driven to be loved at all costs. And in those intimate moments, I did feel loved. I own it all.

I claim both my ignorance and my willfulness. I believe we all go through a sexual rite of passage. Most of us remember it as either shameful or wonderful or maybe we do not remember it at all. At the time it happens, we might not think of it as a rite of passage. It's not purposeful like in some cultures where a person comes of age and is taken through some sort of ritual that has nothing to do with sex. I'm only speaking of a sexual rite of passage here and I believe mine began with my older man. From that point, I believe that experience continued as my go-to map as to how I would express myself sexually. I never questioned it nor was I conscious of it until I really began to dissect my life in my studies to become a practitioner and minister of New Thought. The first year of practitioner studies is titled *How Life Got to Be the Way It Is*. That was when I had to finally face it all and ask myself some tough questions. I believe it is important for every person to do this. For women, it is of the utmost importance as they are the caretakers of all of us due to their very nature.

Iya Omi Tola in *A Tantric Life* wrote this:

> All men and women come into this world
> through the womb of women and are in their
> duty of care during infancy. The mother is
> their first contact with the world and first ex-
> posure to learning. So, by nature, women are
> the teachers of the world and by this natural
> role they have a responsibility to humanity to
> evolve themselves. If a person does not fulfill
> their personal inner work first, then it is impos-
> sible to give anything to other people as logi-
> cally, no one can give something one has never
> had.

It would take me a while before I really evolved myself. I
spoke with a woman who was of Jewish heritage and much
older than me. She grew up pre-World War II. As I sat before
her, I could feel both her delight in my questions and her
willingness to be truthful. Her feelings about sexuality and
her history with her parents were similar to my past. "We just
didn't talk about that," she confided. "We figured it out on
our own and confided in our girlfriends." I gleaned one thing
from our conversation for certain. In her culture, premarital
sex was a no-no and would more than likely result in a forced
marriage. I was touched by her honesty. I was also moved by
her feeling of sacredness for our bodies and of the intimate
act of sex. I identified with her because our family didn't
talk about it either; we also had to discover it on our own.

I also understood about being forced into marriage because my own father tried to force my boyfriend into marrying me when he found out we had engaged in sex.

My conversation with this woman inspired me to do a little research on Judaism and sex. I listened to an interview on *Judaism's Perspective on Sexuality* with Rabbi Mark Wildes and Rabbi Ezra Cohen. They speak about Rabbi Dr. Norman Lamb's book, *A Hedge of Roses*. Lamb describes the post-Freudian period's view of sexuality as stripped of its sacredness and seen purely as a biological pleasure. It was no different than the paganism practiced in ancient Rome. "Today's morality is the old morality in disguise." He goes on to write that during the ancient Roman period of paganism, sex was practiced as a primal urge and sanctity of pleasure. "We have to eat, go to the bathroom and we have bodily sexual urges, so we mate." Lamb calls the modern period, "the Renaissance of paganism." This new morality is detrimental both to the family unit and Judaism. "What feels good, do it!" The opposite is the puritanical viewpoint where sex is negated. Abstinence is required. This is a reaction to paganism and sexual promiscuity. "Christianity calls sex the original sin and celibacy before marriage is required. Repression is the highest ideal."

Since we are all part of the collective consciousness throughout history, it makes sense that sex would be stored in our psyche as dirty and wrong unless performed in the marriage chamber. It becomes black and white. Sex is either all good or all bad. I can see the confusion that this viewpoint, compounded by a lack of mentorship and education, would play upon our psyche.

The Rabbi Cohen continued:

> Judaism rejects both views. In the Kabala it says that God's presence only inhabits a home when a man is married and cohabits it with his wife and they are intimate with each other. Procreation is demanded by the Torah. Sex is valued even without procreation. "It is not good for man to be alone." We must have a mate to be totally fulfilled. The man is to provide food, clothing and satisfaction for his wife. When the woman is menstruating (sex is prohibited), and it is considered a time of sexual tension and a time of working on other parts of their relationship. In the Book of Holiness, the sexual act is elevated and sanctified. Sex is a way of giving to each other and showing commitment to each other. Couples should first make a commitment to each other and use sexuality to strengthen that bond, not the opposite.

When analyzing the story of Genesis and Adam and Eve, Ezra Cohen explained, "It doesn't say Adam had sex with Eve, but that he knew her. Y'dah is the Hebrew word for knowledge." He goes on to say that "sharing consciousness and knowing come first. Not just sex."

So it seems in Judaism, sex is sanctified but only in marriage. From my friend's point of view, this is true. However, she still said that she received little instruction about this. I have yet to have a conversation with anyone in my generation that had that instruction from their parents.

I wonder if they ever thought about the fact that they didn't prepare us in any way for any of it. I wonder if they realized they left us alone to discover it for ourselves. When my own mother found out that I was on birth control pills, instead of confronting me, she took a picture of me from her scrapbook and put it inside the pill box. This was her covert way of telling me she knew. No conversation ever ensued and I was surely not going to start one. I was scared but she was probably even more scared because she knew what my father would do if he found out.

I was seventeen when I got my first birth control pills. I don't remember how I got permission, but I do remember the doctor coming into the room, stripping the sheet from my naked body, and telling me in these exact words, "Birth control and modesty don't go together." I shudder when I think back on these experiences. I also shudder at the fact that I just accepted them without saying anything to anyone. However, it makes sense as I probably didn't want anyone to know that I was having sex, let alone using the pill.

Looking back to my affair with my older man, I see now, over fifty years later, that although I called it love, I had no idea what that was. Love equaled any kind of specialness I felt. I was a clueless young girl finding her way through the forest of puberty by herself. I'm thinking of the story of Red Riding Hood meeting the Wolf. In an essay entitled *Young Women and Wolves: Themes of Sexuality and Identity* in Charles Perrault's *Little Red Riding Hood* and Angela Carter's *The Company of Wolves,* Mia Samardzic, writes this:

In his work, Perrault consistently refers to the young girl as Little Red Riding Hood. She is given this name upon receiving a little red hood made by her grandmother, an item that holds significant figurative meaning. The hood is symbolic of Little Red Riding Hood's virginity, serving in the protection of what Perrault describes as her "innocence." In removing the cape during her encounter with the wolf, Little Red Riding Hood rids herself of this innocence, allowing for the loss of her sexual purity. In addition, because the hood "... became her so well ...," when it is done away with, Little Red Riding Hood loses a vital part of her identity. As her name shows, the young girl was defined by the hood and becomes "naked" when it is cast aside. This exposure ultimately leads to her demise, as she immediately becomes vulnerable to the threat of the wolf and is violently swallowed whole. Through this depiction, Perrault gives the impression that maturing girls who let go of their "innocence" fall apart; not only by ruining their sexual purity, but by undermining their overall integrity as human beings. This overlying message acts as a warning for young girls to protect their virginity, preserving both the innocence and worth that makes up their moral identity.

These are the messages handed down to us through fables, stories, mythology, religion, and from authority figures throughout the ages. The message is clear: loss of purity for women equals death on many levels. Does one have to feel bad for the rest of their lives because they lost that purity through losing their virginity? It seems harsh, and many struggle with this.

My rite of passage with my older man colored the rest of my sexual life until I consciously explored its impact on me. I was not blameless but I should also not condemn myself for losing my innocence at such an integral time in my development. In our philosophy of the Science of Mind and Spirit, I would label me "ignorant." By ignorance, I mean that I didn't know who I was. I didn't know my identity as Divine. I also didn't know what I wanted. I was a person looking for acceptance. Sex became my answer to gain that approval. I am not negating that someone older who should have known better took advantage of my ignorance. What of him? I suspect that he also lacked the mentorship he needed and so the pattern continued.

At one point in my relationship with David, he broke up with me. His reasoning was that he wanted a life that didn't include a serious relationship. He wasn't ready. I'm sure many young relationships go through this breakup phase, some permanently. I was devastated. As he stood in the back of my church with me telling me it was over, ironically at the same time, a wedding was going on inside the sanctuary. This added to the drama and rejection I was feeling.

After the breakup, feeling lost and not knowing what to do next, I went to my girlfriends for sympathy. To help me get over it, one of my best friends set me up with her brother. I agreed because my only feeling at the time was that "I need love. I've been rejected! Where can I turn?" The first date with my friend's brother ended in a kiss in his car. The taste of cigarette smoke on his breath and the fact that I was still in love with David ended that brief encounter. I remember running from the car.

Less than two weeks after our breakup, David asked to meet me so he could return some things to me. I chose to meet him provocatively dressed. It was definitely not an unconscious choice. I knew how he felt about having sex with me. I knew how he felt about my body. I dressed myself to lure him back. I did get him back. However, I never questioned this part of myself. I just continued to get more and more involved with him until one day, I found myself married to him.

A few months before we made the decision to get married, I went to visit my Aunt Lucile in Washington. While I was away, David had a quick fling with one of my girlfriends. He admitted it to me right away and said nothing happened besides a little fondling and a kiss. I was devastated, but not enough to leave him. Instead I asked my aunt to take some naked photos of me to send to him to let him know I was the one he wanted. As I write this, I must keep reminding myself that I was only an eighteen-year-old girl who knew little about relationships and love.

Sex continued to be a huge portion of my relationship with David. I didn't mind. I liked sex. We were great friends too. We had so much fun together but I would have to say that sex was our glue. Our spiritual life didn't exist, or it was forced. We joined a church to have some sense of a foundation for our children. I don't regret anything about my life with David. He was a good man. He supported me through many of my quests for artistic fulfillment and I am ever appreciative of this. He was an amazing father and for that I am ever grateful. As I continued to search for my red dress, which I didn't even know I was missing, I found myself married at the age of eighteen.

Part II - The Unconscious Life

Until you make the unconscious conscious, it will direct your life and you will call it destiny. ~Carl Jung

Chapter 8

A Bride Before Her Time

*You are the most beautiful bride there ever could
be. Don't let anyone else tell you otherwise.*

~Selena Gomez

I titled this chapter *A Bride Before Her Time* because
I married at such a young age. I didn't feel young. I
was supporting myself, had my own apartment, and was
living a life I believed to be happy and fulfilling. I believe
my upbringing ingrained in me the notion that I was destined for marriage. Just as deciding to have sex felt right,
marriage seemed the logical next step. I never considered
alternatives. Perhaps I'm making it sound like a cold-heart-
ed choice, but it wasn't. I was in love and wanted nothing
more than to marry this man. David, on the other hand,
was hesitant about marriage and openly expressed his concerns. He dreamed of sailing with the Merchant Marines
and eventually becoming a millionaire, aspirations he feared
marriage would hinder. I wasn't thinking about becoming a
millionaire or anything besides the desire to be married and
to have children. That is what I was born for after all.

Because of David's concerns and aspirations, it didn't look plausible we would be married anytime soon. Then, due to the absence of sailing opportunities in the early 1970s and a promising job offer he received in New Jersey, marriage suddenly became the right choice. I vividly recall when he received that offer. We were in New Mexico with his family. I feared losing him to the sea. If he had chosen the Merchant Marines life, maintaining our relationship and the prospect of marriage would have been challenging. Although it's irrelevant now, reflecting on these moments helps me understand the evolution of our twenty-seven-year relationship.

I left home to escape my father's control and I intentionally sought someone completely unlike him. I found that person in my husband-to-be. David was kind and loving. Although I didn't recognize it then, in many ways he became another father figure. Highly intelligent, he often seemed to know more than I did and I relied on him to make decisions. For instance, I wanted children immediately—wasn't that what women did? David sought financial security first. We agreed that children would follow our first home purchase. I was learning that marriage was a compromise.

Looking back, I do not regret marrying young. I believe it was the perfect decision for me, leading to significant personal growth. I see now that there are no mistakes, only choices made without full awareness of their consequences. Ernest Holmes wrote this about mistakes in the *Science of Mind* and I have often found it helpful.

Suppose someone says, "I have made a lot of mistakes in my life, I had opportunities I did not grasp." Every person has this feeling at some time in his life. This is a direct belief that there is but one opportunity which comes to a person and if he does not take it, he will have no more. ... It is not that we have made no mistakes, but if the belief in the necessity of mistakes stays in the consciousness, then there is bound to be a repetition. It is scientific practice to declare that there have been no mistakes in man's consciousness, and that if there have been, they are now wiped out. There are none in the Divine Plan, and there is no plan for man other than the Divine plan.

Ernest Holmes is saying that there is always another chance. There is no finality to opportunity for success. Although I married young, I can say I had no missed opportunities. What I chose for myself actualized itself even in marriage. I didn't know these Science of Mind principles at the time but I can see in retrospect that they were in place in my life, as they are for all of us. We might not know about the "Divine Plan," but the Universe always has our back. What does this mean? From my studies of New Thought Philosophy, it means that the Creative Power that birthed the Universe is the Power of Life. That is Its impulsion. The Creative Power works through each of us at the capacity of our recognition of it. We are always moving toward life even with our setbacks and side tracks.

I acted based on the level of my eighteen-year-old consciousness and my experiences up to that point. I didn't know that there was a Creative Power within me that was propelling my life forward. If I had, I might have made different decisions. I was still working from past programming unconsciously. My brain, which was wired from that programming, longed for marriage, care, and freedom—all which David provided. The fact that we did not share spiritual beliefs did not seem important at the time. As I grew up and became more spiritually conscious, our lack of partnership in this area would eventually make a big difference in our relationship.

David and I were married on December 31, 1971, in our New Jersey apartment, decorated with fluorescent posters which were popular at that time. We were joined by my aunt, my grandma, and a few of David's New Mexico friends. The only person who attended from David's family was his twin sister. His parents gave some excuse about not being able to afford the trip to New Jersey. I still wonder about that but I never pursued what the real reason might have been. David let me know that he picked the December 31 date for the wedding so we could file our taxes jointly. That was the first time I was considered a loss on our tax returns. I didn't think of it at the time as something derogatory. It just seemed like a good way to deal with our taxes. David did our finances and I never got involved. Being a tax loss would continue to be an emblem that I would wear throughout our marriage.

I also didn't think anything about the fact that David forgot to get our wedding license for our Unitarian minister to sign or that he was suffering from stomach flu on the day of our wedding. We picked the Unitarian minister because it was a spiritual philosophy, according to David, that wasn't religious. I'm not sure why we didn't just go to a Justice of the Peace. I think we wanted that intimate wedding in our apartment with friends and family. I agreed to David's request that the word *God* not be mentioned in our wedding vows. As I look back on it, I admit how strange it was that I never protested any of this nor did I ask any questions. I just went along with it, happy to be getting married. I made lasagna for the wedding dinner and agreed to it all.

My early married years were filled with sex, fun, and work. At times, spirituality did slip into our conversations. Discussions about Jesus, whom I still believed in as my Savior, were off-limits for David. He dismissed the Bible as fairytales. I remember crying silently, not from disconnection, but because I feared for his salvation. I was still very much influenced by my childhood Catholic teachings. I worshipped Jesus in private. I initially dismissed the spiritual differences between David and me as unimportant. I had a husband who was fun, adored me, and provided security. He was hardworking whereas I was still exploring my potential. I managed our home and worked in retail, seizing every opportunity I could to earn money. When David needed to travel for business, I followed him, putting my education on hold, guided by my instinct to stay close to him. In the first year of our marriage, David's commitments to the Merchant Marines required him to be away for one month each year.

I despised being alone. I had no family relationships. I had few friends.

You might be wondering why I had no family relationships. Let me step back a moment. My relationship with my parents worsened significantly after David and I began having sex. At seventeen when my father discovered our relationship, he disowned me, initiating over two years of painful silence. This silence even extended to my job at the hospital where he practiced. We would walk down the same corridor and not even glance at each other. My brothers and sisters were forbidden to talk to me. When David and I decided to marry, I naïvely invited my estranged family to the wedding. This caused another wedge in our relationship because David and I were not married in a Catholic Church. My Aunt Lucile, attempting to mend relations, took a piece of our wedding cake to my family. Soon after, I received a beautifully wrapped package from my parents containing the cake, a symbolic gesture of the pain I had caused my family. I remember opening that beautiful package thinking perhaps my parents had forgiven me for falling from grace. The shock and pain I felt only further instilled in me how bad I really was. But I was not ready to change the situation, nor did I know how. Therapy would become essential for me eventually, but at the time, I just buried these painful feelings and instead focused on my happiness with David. I was fulfilling my father's negative prophecies about me but I was content to be away from my childhood home.

Years later, after divorcing David and planning to marry Patrick, my mother suggested a Catholic wedding, claiming my first marriage was invalid without the Catholic Church's blessing. By then, Patrick and I were members of a Religious Science Church and Patrick politely declined.

Eventually I reconciled with my parents. Encouraged by my best friend and colleague at the time, I visited my parents' home on Mother's Day. This led to a poignant but complicated forgiveness from my father. He never forgot the past and neither did I. He would often say, "I forgive, but I do not forget." I continued to carry that metaphorical scarlet letter fastened to my chest by the glue of my guilt in disappointing my parents. Eventually, I would accept this part of my identity. It would take time but I would learn to embrace the totality of my life, red dress and all.

At this time, where was my red dress? I most definitely didn't even know what it was. I had no concept of true deep respect and love for myself. My red dress was buried in my idyllic and naïve beliefs about marriage and love.

Chapter 9

Ten Years a Mormon

Each time a woman stands up for herself, without knowing its possibility, without claiming it, she stands up for all women.

~Maya Angelou

In 1975, David and I and our first born moved to Farmington, New Mexico. It was David's dream to go back to his roots. He grew up in Albuquerque but Farmington would suffice for now. We converted to Mormonism, joining the Church of Jesus Christ of Latter-day Saints. This affiliation is connected to the Salt Lake City Mormons who consider themselves the one-true Church, not to be confused with the many offshoot sects of the original Church founded by Joseph Smith in the 1800s. For brevity, I will refer to myself as Mormon and the Church as Mormonism.

We were drawn to Mormonism because we were looking for a stable life's philosophy for our daughter who was five months old at the time. Up to this point, after leaving the Catholic Church seven years prior, I felt free in my physicality. I didn't judge myself. I dressed the way I wanted to dress. If I wanted to sunbathe nude in my secluded yard, I

did. I nursed my baby modestly, but anywhere I wanted to
nurse her, I did. I was like my little daughter who loved to be
naked and free out in the yard in her swimming pool. I was
once again that young girl who laid in the snow looking up
at the blue, blue sky and feeling only oneness. My red dress
consciousness, although unconscious, was alive in what I
perceived as freedom from religious dogma and my father's
opinion of me.

People often ask me how I could have become a Mormon.
It didn't fit my personality or my sense of spiritual and physical freedom. The answer is multi-dimensional. Some of it
has to do with the philosophy of past lives which I won't
go into here. In the conditional world it made total sense.
Think about it. I was living in Farmington, alone without
family or friends. I was looking for community and we were
seeking a way of life in which to bring up our daughter.
Religion seemed logical, even to David. I still longed to have
some sense of spirituality in my relationship with David.
Mormonism was just that. It was family-oriented and com-
munity- driven. For a young twenty-three-year-old like me,
isolated from family and friends in the middle of a town of
27,000 people, it makes total sense now. In Mormonism, I
had an instantaneous family. In the depths of my spiritual
evolution and my evolution as a soul, there was much more.
I would discover this much later.

As a Mormon, I was like Eve in the Garden of Eden who
discovered her nakedness. I had allowed myself a brief time
of freedom but my unresolved issues with authority and
patriarchy raised their head again. Every detail of my guilt
and upbringing would come to the foreground through my

experience in Mormonism. Every one of my beliefs about myself would be tested again. This is what we can all expect until we become conscious and decide to take responsibility for our lives. We live our subconscious beliefs over and over again. I'm sure you've heard the phrase, "Wherever you go, there you are." That would be me, appearing and reappearing for a very long time.

Before joining the Mormon Church, we had to go through an interview process. I disclosed that I had committed adultery because I had engaged in an affair with a married man when I was a teenager. I remember the bishop letting me know that it wasn't adultery on my part because I wasn't married. It didn't make total sense but it relieved me of some of my guilt. I accepted the words of this "authority." As a Mormon, that is what one did. When an authority such as a bishop or stake president (always a man), said something was so, you didn't question it.

For example, it was the belief, at least in the branch that we attended, that any kind of sex outside of the missionary position was considered a sin and should not be indulged in. During one of our interviews, we were questioned about our sex life. I remember the answer my husband gave to the question, "Have you ever engaged in deviated sex?" These were the exact words the bishop used. My husband asked, "What do you mean by deviated sex?" The bishop answered quite quickly, "Well ... oral sex, or anal sex ..." The question was directed at my husband, not me. Women are subservient to men in the Mormon faith. My husband answered quite firmly, "Well, yes, we do." The bishop was not uncomfortable in his answer. He went on to let David know that this was not acceptable.

When we left the bishop's office that day, we decided that no one need know what went on in our bedroom. However, I must admit that as a young twenty-three-year-old woman who still believed in an outside judgmental God and who respected authority, I was confused as to what was right in God's eyes. It was still very much a formative time in my life when I was trying to find out what I believed and what I stood for. Although I claimed to be free to choose my life, and I had done so up to this point, I still looked to the outside and authority figures for my worth.

As my years as a Mormon continued, I was fraught with conflicting feelings about their views about relationships, sex, and so much more. I studied as much of the Mormon history that was available. During the days of Brigham Young, men were allowed to have more than one wife while women were to remain monogamous. The Mormons abolished polygamy during the 1800s. They say they did away with it because of a revelation by the Church President at that time. However, the revelation came after much turmoil with the government because polygamy was against civil law in the United States. What follows is a recent announcement by the Church of Jesus Christ of Latter-day Saints on polygamy:

> Today, the practice of polygamy is strictly prohibited in the Church. No one can practice it and remain a member. In 1998, Church

President Gordon B. Hinckley announced, "I wish to state categorically that this Church has nothing whatever to do with those practicing polygamy. They are not members of this Church. Most of them have never been members. They are in violation of the civil law... If any of our members are found to be practicing plural marriage, they are excommunicated, the most serious penalty the Church can impose."

What I was taught as a Mormon is that, although polygamy is against civil law, it is still considered a Law of Heaven. There are still branches who do practice polygamy, but not the Salt Lake Mormons who considered themselves the true Church. You can read more about this decree here... http://tiny.cc/soxwzz

I spent a lot of time thinking about the contradictions that Mormonism presented to me concerning sex and life in general. I was constantly adjusting and denying what I was feeling. My red dress was hung in the closet during those days. I turned a blind eye to what I didn't agree with. There was so much good in having built-in family and friends that it made up for any of my conflicting feelings.

Still I kept butting my head up against some of the Mormon theology that just didn't make sense to my logical mind or my spirit. I remember nursing my baby during the church service. I was very discreet, covering myself up, but someone saw me and reported it to the bishop. I was called in and told it was not proper to nurse my baby in public and that I should go into the restroom or somewhere private. Something within me did not feel right about this but I let it go and accepted the bishop's reprimand. At the time, I was close to going through the auspicious temple ceremony. I surely didn't want to mess up that opportunity. It was very important to me. In the temple ceremony ritual, the husband, wife, and children are joined together for eternity. It was this tenet that drew me to Mormonism to begin with. I loved my husband and my children and the idea of an eternal union was comforting to my young mind.

While I was a Mormon, I entered the theater world as an actress and singer. Once again, my reputation came to the foreground at the Church. When people saw me kissing other men on stage, I had to answer for myself. I was asked to stop but this time I didn't agree. I rebelled instead. Acting and theater were important to me. My husband didn't mind so why should I stop. Accepting my role as a "loose" woman seemed to be my lot and I consciously took it on and went on with my involvement in theater. My friends let me know that there was whispering behind my back. What was it in my consciousness that continually put me in this battle of self: whore and saint. Now it is obvious to me I was still wrestling with my upbringing and the unconscious beliefs I had about myself. I was still playing out my self-cast role as whore.

It was finally time to go to the Temple where my husband and I would be given the holy garments to wear. The wearing of the garments reminds one of the covenants that he/she makes in the Temple. According to Mormonism, the garment has a Biblical reference. The Church of Jesus Christ of Latter-day Saints website reads:

When Adam and Eve were expelled from the Garden of Eden, our Heavenly Father did not abandon them. Instead, He instructed them on His plan of happiness and salvation. He entered into covenants with them, and then gave them "coats of skins" to remind them of those covenants (Genesis 3:21; Moses 4:27).

When the Lord brought Israel out of Egypt, He again entered into covenants with His chosen people. He also provided instruction regarding their garments, specifically how their clothes could remind them of the commandments (Numbers 15:37-41). For Aaron and others who would officiate in the tabernacle, Moses was commanded to "make holy garments . . . for glory and for beauty . . . that [they] may minister unto me." (Exodus 28:2-3).

At the time, I gladly accepted these garments. I was very dedicated to the Mormon Church and its precepts even though the contradictions persisted. I just buried them where they weren't as glaringly obvious. It's amazing how we can deny our intuition and succumb to the outside pull unconsciously, making it okay in our mind even against our own will.

After the temple ceremony, my wardrobe changed to capped sleeved shirts and longer, high- collared dresses. I willingly gave up my spaghetti straps and bikinis and did my best to fit in. Many people think Mormons do not take off their garments when having sex and are not allowed to go swimming because of having to wear garments all the time. This is not true.

I became a woman with secrets. I couldn't tell anyone about the garments or what they meant. The temple ceremony was a secret, not to be disclosed to anyone. I still had friends outside the Faith and I couldn't have honest conversations with them. Unfortunately, religion can create separation when it should be bringing people together. This seems to be something that has never changed in our world.

After I reconciled with my family, I now had something else to separate us—my new religion. Although my parents were grateful I'd found religion, they weren't quite sure about Mormonism. My father especially couldn't stand the fact that I couldn't drink wine. He'd jokingly put the wine glass under my nose, trying to tempt me. My mother finally told him to stop. "You sound like Satan, Rocco!" she scolded.

The secretive nature of wearing these garments was literally a physical separation between me, my sensuality, and my friendships with my non-Mormon friends. I remember going to my non-Mormon best girlfriend's house to do a photo shoot with her for a theatrical headshot. She pulled my dress down on my shoulder. I responded by quickly yanking my dress up. She was stunned at my modesty. Was I the same person she'd spent her teenage years with sunbathing nude and skinny-dipping? I couldn't explain my secret garments to her. She respected my privacy and didn't ask. She gave me a confusing look and went on with the photo shoot.

I didn't know it at the time but I wouldn't last long under these restrictions. I was already in so much inner turmoil. Because I loved the family and community aspects that came with being Mormon so much, I continued to resist my conflicting feelings between being the sensual me and adhering to the Mormon standard of being a woman. What I experienced is that Mormon women are put up on a pedestal as pure and virtuous, but in all other areas they are not equal to men. They are held in high regard but only to serve God in the ways specified by the rules of the Church; rules made by the men of course. All this coincided with my subconscious battle between who I thought I should be and who I desired to be. Which was the true me? It would take a while before I discovered that person. At times in this Mormon journey, I think I even forgot I had a red dress. It was hidden in the closet of my subconscious, mixed up with my guilt and my strong desire to please others.

One of my times of freedom from Mormon dogma came on a houseboat vacation on Lake Powell in Arizona. I was accompanied by several good friends, couples and singles, none of them Mormons. I'm not sure how I justified my behavior on this trip. Perhaps it was because I knew no one would ever know. As we were leaving the dock, the wife of the couple that invited us told me she was taking off her top and that most of the trip would be spent half-clothed. She knew I was a Mormon and wanted to let me know in a fun and daring way that she wasn't going to let my religious beliefs stop her from freely expressing herself. My answer to her was to take off my own top.

What I thought of as the real Rita was back for those fourteen days! I found my red dress in my nakedness. Who was the real Rita? I didn't think about it consciously at that time but now I can see that what I considered the real Rita didn't have taboos regarding her body. She felt comfortable being naked. She liked her body and was proud of it. She felt comfortable in sexy dresses and feeling uninhibited. At the same time, there was always that outside observer, the critic, the judge, the Rita who knew that she was naked and maybe that wasn't all right. Was I a hedonist? Hedonism is defined as "the doctrine that pleasure or happiness is the sole or chief good in life." (Merriam-Webster Dictionary). Maybe I was, but I doubt hedonists carried as much guilt as I always did.

Ten years into my life as a Mormon, the restrictions and contradictions between me and the dogma of the Church became emotionally draining and overwhelming. I was caught between two worlds and my red dress of freedom was calling me back. The call got louder and louder every day. My earlier experiences with my liberal friends and my life in the theater were urging me to freedom. My best friends were gay and that was definitely not a Mormon precept. I couldn't imagine that these beautiful men I knew were destined to go to hell. Something was not right in my spiritual, logical mind. To the Mormons, I was the woman who was a little too free. There were always whispers in the corridors and reprimands here and there. I did my best to comply and be the good "Molly Mormon." This is a term used for the perfect Mormon woman who was never quite as perfect as she seemed. My red dress certainly didn't fit in. Finally, I couldn't hold Rita back any more.

By now I had three children. My youngest was five years old. In the course of one night, we left the church on our own accord. We went from being full-tithing and temple-going Mormons to suddenly leaving the church. Of course, it is never quite as sudden as it seems to others as it is to the one who has been struggling. This final step came after ten years of denying the deep suppression I was feeling.

How did it happen? One night when the pain of my values and beliefs were in direct conflict with my actions as a Mormon became overbearing, I knelt and prayed with my husband. I still believed in a Heavenly Father. No one could take that away from me, not even a judgmental and rigid church. As we finished our prayer, pleading to know what to do, the Bible fell open to a passage that let me know we were not to be deceived. It went on to say that we would not find God in a temple or in the desert. (Salt Lake was a desert at one time.) Then it stated clearly that the coming of the Son of Man would be as the sun rising in the east to the west. Here is the passage from Matthew 24-27:

> For there shall arise false Christs, and false prophets, and shall shew great signs and wonders; insomuch that, if it were possible, they shall deceive the very elect. Behold, I have told you before. Wherefore if they shall say unto you, Behold, he is in the desert; go not forth: behold, he is in the secret chambers; believe it

not. For as the lightning cometh out of the east, and shineth even unto the west; so shall also the coming of the Son of man be.

Since Satan did sit in the Mormon Temple and everything else in that passage matched up in our eager minds, I got up from my knees and went straight to my typewriter (we didn't have a computer in those days) and typed a letter asking that our children's names and ours be removed from the records of the Church. The Mormon hierarchy must have been shocked. I can only imagine the gossip in those secret church chambers. We were the model Mormons for ten years, not to mention the 10 percent of our gross income that they would lose.

After that night, the Mormon Church pursued us for two years and we were finally excommunicated which was "the most serious penalty the Church can impose." I remember the night the Mormon elders knocked on our door unannounced. They gave us one last chance to come back to the fold. It was very dramatic. We told them our decision was final. They let us know, in no uncertain terms, they were shaking the dirt from their shoes, which is a Bible quote given by Jesus to the apostles if someone rejected the gospel. "If any household or town refuses to welcome you or listen to your message, shake its dust from your feet as you leave." (Matthew 10:14 New Living Translation 14)

The elders severely reprimanded us. They told us we had turned against Jesus, the Savior. They explained that because we rejected His true church, we outwardly rejected Jesus.

Not only would we be damned for the rest of our lives, we would forever be under Satan's power. These statements coming from what I considered to be authoritative figures shot straight into my subconscious. Therapy would be necessary in my future. I might have decided to leave the Church but it didn't mean I felt good about it. The undercurrents of guilt and feeling I was wrong still haunted me. Would I be condemned by God forever? Although I was relieved to finally be freed from Mormon dogma and felt I had made the right decision, I took their words deeply into my heart. That little girl within me was scared. She had displeased Daddy once again.

While all this was happening, I was studying for the role of Susannah in an opera by the same name written by American composer, Carlisle Floyd. I thoroughly identified with this character. Susannah was a sensuous woman in a small southern town. She was ostracized by her church community as being too sexual and a menace. The story is based on a story from the Apocrypha. The elders of her town find Susannah bathing naked in a stream on her property. At first, the elders are sexually turned on by the sight of her. Then, quite suddenly they turn against themselves for their lustful thoughts and openly take it out on her.

I have no idea whether any of the Mormon elders were turned on by me but I do know that for years I was reprimanded for any behavior that was not in congruence with the role of a woman, wife, and mother. My Mormon days affected me emotionally and mentally. I spent the next few years in therapy to heal from what I consider the brainwashing I went through in the Temple. Picture this: A gorgeous but evil Satan appears on the screen and tells you that if you break any of the covenants you made in the Temple, you are condemned forever. It would take me several years to mentally free myself.

It was through past-life therapy that I came to understand much about myself and my pull toward Mormonism. Past-life therapy brought deep understanding to my life and many of the conflicts I had regarding relationships. The past-life story was centered around a sexual encounter I had with a Mormon elder, very similar to what happened to Susannah. In this past life, I was raped. I kept that rape a secret until my dying day because I had convinced myself it was my fault. Why? Because I had danced with him at a local community dance. My condemnation by the Church at that time surrounded my daughter and my inability to go to her wedding because I had refused the join the Mormon Church. This elder had come to my house to convince me to convert. He then took advantage of me. During this present life, it became clear through the past-life therapy, I had joined the Church to pay that debt to my daughter. Many of the characters from that life reassembled themselves in this life. That past-life daughter was my first-born daughter in this life. As you might recall, we joined the Mormon Church to create a stable life for her. There were many other synchronicities that I couldn't explain at the time but became clear during the past-life therapy. I can see that the sexual residue and guilt I felt about myself was still there in this life. In fact, my husband in this life said this to me when we left. "I was waiting for you to come to your senses. I left a long time ago. I was just doing this for you."

When it finally came down to leaving the Church, the last word was mine and my decision to end the horrible conflicts I was feeling. My youngest daughter who was five at the time and quite outspoken, said this when we told the children we were leaving, "So, you're saying they are all liars!" She is still astute to this day. Thank you for that, Laura! You get it!

As a Mormon, I was told I was exalted in the "eyes of God" just for being a woman. To be able to bear children was a gift from Heavenly Father, never to be denied. I knew many women who had seven or eight or even ten children. I knew one woman who had seventeen children! At the same time, there was a limit to a woman's exaltation in that she could only move up in her station as a man would permit. The men chose and decided everything and the women followed. How perfect this fit my upbringing. However, something was stirring within me and the constraints of being a Mormon woman would not allow whatever that was to be birthed. It was that call to what was still unknown. I was still running without a compass.

I do not want to dismiss my ten years as a Mormon as just a dark time in my life. I found a lot of joy in being Mormon, especially in the early years. I learned about the power of community and how a community cares for its own. I learned the Law of Tithing which I still practice today. I practiced faith and trust in God even during difficult times. Being a Mormon brought much good to my life, but like many journeys in life sometimes we, in the words of a song by Billy Barnes and Peter Matz, may have "stayed too long at the fair."

A friend of mine and I were just discussing this recently. Why do we stay too long in a relationship or experience? We can be miserable and yet we just keep going. We make excuses. We give second chances. We deny our feelings. My friend and I both came to the same conclusion. It was all about our own individual evolution, our self-knowingness, and self-confidence. The more we become in tune with ourselves and are fearless in admitting what we really want from life, the more we grow into our true selves, these "stays at the fair" shorten. Eventually we spot these unhealthy experiences before we even embark upon them. Until then, I believe we experience life by trial and error. We are never lost as long as we are willing to change. I have another friend who, when deciding whether to enter a new relationship or experience, asks this of herself: "Potential for drama or no potential for drama?" This is something I am still working on to this day.

Chapter 10

Free and Curious

*My sexuality is not an inferior trait that needs
to be chaperoned by emotionalism or morality.*

~Alice Bag

After leaving the Mormon church, I felt free and curious. I was thirty-three years old and suddenly I had no restrictions to prevent me from my explorations of life and relationships. I was married and a mother but that part of me, that young colt freed from religious dogma, was open to experience life. I proudly wore my own version of my red dress.

As I look back on it, I feel that my thirties were the teenage puberty that I never had the opportunity to experience. I grew up before my time. Think of it. I literally had no dating life as a teenager and I experienced a sexual rite of passage that was most definitely out of the ordinary. Then I fell into marriage at age eighteen. I never experienced those years that I have witnessed my own children and other children experiencing. I'm speaking of that time when you are wondering who you are and what sex is all about. You experience friendships and the ending of friendships. You fall in and out of love. I would explore all of this in my thirties. What would become of me? If the Mormons had witnessed me during this decade, they would most certainly have ascertained that I had fallen under Satan's power.

It all began with my intense intrigue with polygamy and polyamorous relationships which followed me into my ex-Mormon life. I understand it wasn't a true precept of the Mormon Church but many engaged in it, beginning with Brigham Young. After some research, I understand that it wasn't a precept of the original *Book of Mormon* or the *Doctrine and Covenants,* but from what I was taught, "celestial marriage" was an order of Heaven. Perhaps I was intrigued because of my own desires but I deeply questioned why women couldn't have multiple partners. It didn't seem fair to me. I mean if men could have more than one wife, why couldn't women have more than one husband or more than one lover? Some would say it was because men could impregnate more than one woman at the same time but it had to be more than biological. Like much of the Mormon faith, I believed that it was about maintaining men's superiority over women. That didn't sit well with me in my post-Mormon days. I was trying to break free into my power as a woman. I didn't think of the consequences of my actions. I just wanted to explore. I wanted to be free.

David was never against experimenting in our marriage. He welcomed it and often instigated it. If he were to look back on it, he would say he did it for me, but why was he the one who always suggested the sexual incident? In retrospect, we never would have said that we were unsatisfied with each other. We never talked to other couples about it but I wonder now how many couples go through this period of experimentation. I'm now finding there are more than I knew of at that time. Again, we didn't talk about those things. What happened inside a marriage was a private thing.

This is how this experimental period of our marriage began. As is very common in theatrical life, I would sometimes develop crushes on my leading men or another man in the production. I've heard a term used for this—"showmance." During my Mormon days I would never have acted upon these crushes but my husband and I did discuss it. I know it turned him on because it most definitely spiced up our sex life.

Once we left the Mormon church, the field was wide open for experimentation. And I had more time to get involved in local theater productions. I was cast as the lead in numerous shows. On two particular occasions, I developed a crush on my leading man that went further than expected. David would notice it and say something like, "I think you like him." We'd talk about it. I don't know that I would have acted on it, and for the most part, I didn't. Most of the time we just talked about it. However, in these two cases my husband encouraged me, saying it might be fun. He would then invite the person into our bedroom. I'm not saying I was not a partner in this decision. I'm just saying that he instigated it. It happened twice and both times it ended in emotional disasters because I was always hurt in the end. In one of the instances, I was accused of suffocating this person with my intense feelings. In other words, I wanted more than he could give. It wasn't casual sex for me. In fact, I always had to convince myself that I was in love with the person before engaging in sex. How could I be in love? It makes no sense now. I barely knew the person. The first time I believe I was simply curious and wanted to experiment. My husband was always part of it so there were no lies or secrets between us. For those of us who have engaged in theatrical productions, we know that these feelings of closeness are usually fleeting. They are built on the falsity of feelings that are felt between a group of people in a make-believe world. This is not uncommon, but it is usually not lasting.

Before the first relationship ended, the man asked us to go to a retreat with him. I don't remember the name of the group but it was one of those therapy retreats where people disclose their relationships for group discussion. The man we were involved with called me out in front of the group. This was the setting he chose to break up with me. In front of all those people, none of whom I knew, he related what he perceived as my possessiveness. From his perspective, he related the intricacies of the whole relationship. I was mortified and all I could do was defend myself. Everything was pointed at me. The group leader then started to interrogate me about my past. I distinctly remember him asking me, "Did you have two fathers? This is most abnormal. Why do you need a relationship with more than one man?" I didn't know the answers to any of his questions. He never asked David anything. I was the one on display. That was the last day of this three-way relationship and I left that retreat in shame.

I was deeply submerged in my victimhood, pointing my finger outward. I should have been able to look at this relationship for what it was, the simple ending of a sexual relationship. However, I had blown it up into a great love affair. I was sure I was rejected for what I conceived of as not being enough; not being good enough in the bedroom. Was I not sexy enough? Did I not give enough? Of course, it wasn't true. I gave everything. I now know it isn't that I was not enough; the relationship and I were just too much for that person. I had unrealistic expectations of what a three-way relationship could be. I was much too naïve to understand that this was just a fantasy. Instead, I had turned it into something very serious, something I thought would be lasting. No wonder I was so deeply hurt. I still had no idea that I was the one who needed to examine myself and my motives. David and I needed to take a serious look at our relationship, but we didn't. We just moved on.

It didn't take me too long to get over this first relationship before another opportunity presented itself. What was I looking for? In my present spiritual maturity, I now see that I was truly thirsty for more validation of myself as a woman. I disguised it as experimentation in my marriage, denying that there was a peculiar aspect to the way my husband and I were behaving; not in the sense that I was immoral, but peculiar in the sense that I thought I was doing something to enhance my marriage bed. In the end, it severed my marriage. This relationship along with the next one drove me further away from David. Did my marriage end with that first decision to "experiment?" I believe it did. I was too afraid to admit it at the time but something in our relationship from its very beginnings needed attention. Because I had married so young, I never truly got to know myself or what I wanted in a relationship.

I remember going to a retreat led by a past life teacher and author where one of the participants came up to me out of the blue and told me I might consider working on my marriage. He said he was speaking from some psychic hit he was feeling. "I'm just trying to be helpful," he said quietly. I didn't know how to respond. The man walked away quickly. I was pretty stunned by that remark. Maybe there was something about David and me that was visible in the subjective field that only someone with psychic ability could see. Others thought we had the perfect marriage. I believed I loved David and I sometimes wonder what would have happened to us had we not engaged in those three-way relationships. I wonder what would have happened had we just worked on our marriage and ourselves. However, I don't think we were consciously thinking that we needed to do that, not in the way that man meant. I believe at the time we thought what we were doing was fine. There was much about our marriage that was good. That I will never deny. What I know now is that those three-way affairs were assisting us in finding our relationship. During those affairs, we were unconsciously working on our marriage in the most unusual way. We discovered that we were both destined for something else.

The next three-way relationship unfolded two years after the first. I was in a play again and began to develop a friendship with my leading man. It might have been the content of the play, which was highly romantic and passionate, but this time I was convinced that I was deeply in love. I would have done anything for this person, and I did. Once again, David was involved. If someone told me that David was just doing this for me, I would fight vehemently to let them know that it was not the case. My husband was most definitely getting very turned on by these trysts. He was getting even more turned on than the man in our bed.

I'm not sure why this particular man agreed to the relationship. First of all, he was married. Now I know he was a wanderer. I was not the first of his affairs. I remember him saying to David, "I'm only here for her. I'm not interested in anything else." Of course, he was referring to David. This relationship was wild and crazy and heartbreaking and after three years, it abruptly ended with no seeming explanation. He just stopped calling and coming over. I knew the reason. He was married and I believe his wife knew about it. How couldn't she? I really believed that something would eventually come of it. I convinced myself that he loved me. I remember one night as I lay in his arms, he told me that at some specific point in the future when his kids were grown, he would join us. I believed him. I don't know about others who have had affairs with someone who is married, but for me I had convinced myself that he wasn't happy in his marriage and somehow it was okay. I'm not proud of any of this. It's taken me a while to forgive myself.

You are probably wondering where my children were during these trysts. Sometimes they were at friends' houses. Most of the meetings took place somewhere other than our home, or if at our house, very late at night when our children were asleep. I believe the children were unaware of these secret get-togethers. Later, I did share all of this with them. I don't want to leave any question in their minds of who I was and who I have become since.

In analyzing myself, I ask, was I crazy or desperate? I was definitely looking for what I am now calling my red dress in all the wrong places. The end of this second relationship plunged me into a deep darkness which I had to painstakingly pull myself out. I was so devastated that I had to force myself out of bed in the morning. If it weren't for my love for my children, who knows what would have happened to me? I was deeply depressed. I felt lost. I didn't know who I was. David had no idea what to do for me. At the same time, I was getting my master's degree and working as a theater teacher. When I went to work, my feelings got buried and I was fully engaged in what I was doing. When I arrived home, the pain continued deep into my cellular being. I thought I would never get over it but what I explored next rescued me from my misery.

I was introduced to past life therapy. It was the deep healing that I needed. It allowed me to discover the karma that I was unconsciously working out in this life. I was finally able to let go of the patterns that weren't serving me. I am grateful for my past life therapist, Terry. We had some amazing sessions in the late 1980s and into the early 1990s. Even in my past lives, sex was always involved. Those lives always entailed the unrequited kind of love that was shrouded in secrecy and pain. Some even ended in violence. I worked out so much in those sessions with Terry. I came to understand my wounds and heal them. I even found a life where I was one of David's girls in a brothel. That explained some of his eagerness in this life to share me with other men.

Perhaps you don't believe in past lives. For me, it was a huge breakthrough. When you can put the pieces of your past together with an experienced therapist walking you through it, much healing takes place. For one thing, you realize you do not need to repeat the pattern in this life. There is also much forgiveness on all levels. Unless you've experienced past life therapy, you might not understand what I am talking about. Let me explain. First of all, it was the type of therapy where I was the one in control. Upon embarking on the session, I would have some particular aspect of my life or some relationship that I wanted to explore. After being put into an altered state, my therapist asked questions that drew the story out of me. The session would progress in the most surprising ways. If I was making it up, I surely was making it up in the moment, unrehearsed. I often tell myself that I don't care if I made it up or not. The truth is, it allowed me to heal and that is all that matters.

As I analyze that time in my life and these extramarital relationships, both men left because I wanted more from them. They didn't mind the fling, the fun, the sex, but I wanted more—more intimacy, more commitment. It might have been fun to begin with but I would always turn it into a more serious encounter than anyone wanted and I was left brokenhearted. At the time, I didn't see this wanting more as something that was lacking in my relationship with David. Or if I did, I did not admit it. I was behaving without truly thinking of the consequences of my actions.

As I am writing this book, I got word that the man in this last relationship had passed away. I was so amazed at myself and the feelings I still had. I talked about it with my husband Patrick and he totally understood that you just don't stop loving someone. Compounding this, was the fact that much of that relationship and its ending was never resolved. I did a releasing ceremony and wished him well on his eternal journey. I allowed myself to feel my feelings now, some thirty years later.

David's standard answer to all our relationship experimentations, our lives as Mormons, and our life in general was, "I did it for Rita." I ended up feeling like the bad one. Would this haunting feeling that was birthed in my childhood through my father's reprimands and my rite of passage with my older man ever be healed? You might wonder if these feelings about myself came up in my past life therapy. Yes and no. I did work on the feelings of being bad but I do not believe I was ready to forgive myself totally. Not yet. There was more to learn and more to grow through.

If I wanted to assign blame for these choices in our relationship, both David and I were both to blame. However, I was the one who took on the burden of guilt. I was the victim and the perpetrator. In my ignorance of my dissatisfaction with my marriage, I tried to fix it in all the wrong ways. We did eventually go through some therapy but there didn't seem to be an answer that the therapist could find for us besides we needed to stop these extra marital affairs. I remember one therapist just sitting in his chair in judgment and anger. You might wonder why we didn't continue to try to find solutions. Maybe we didn't want to. We just moved on and covered the pain with taking care of our children, working, and superfluous activities. After the second disaster and the emotional pain that ensued, I swore off my ménage à trois lifestyle. It is not an exaggeration to say that I felt somewhat like Jessica Lange, who said at the end of the movie about Frances Farmer, "Life is just going to be a little slower now." In my case, life was going to be a little mundane now. It was better than all the drama, or so I thought.

My past life therapy helped me to understand some of the people with whom I became involved. At the same time, I became very hungry for the New Age movement of the late eighties and early nineties. What I was learning through channeling, crystal healing, and tarot card readings brought me many answers to the whys and wherefores of my life. I began to realize that it wasn't really about the men I loved; it was what they brought out in me—that desperate need to be loved, accepted, and feeling like enough. This is the identity that claimed me for a long time, and still to this day, I must work hard to forgive myself and to realize my beauty and goodness.

My work in New Thought and Science of Mind, which would come much later, assisted me in recognizing my God Self and in accepting what I considered my mistakes as part of my spiritual growth and evolution. I also came to understand that there really were no mistakes and that I was merely evolving and discovering myself, doing the best I could at the time with the knowledge I had. I was also paying the consequences of my actions with mental pain and suffering. Neuroscientist Dr. Joe Dispenza and Science of Mind founder Dr. Ernest Holmes both say, "We are not punished for our sins, but by our sins." Keep in mind that in the New Thought Movement, a sin is not about doing something "evil." It is about missing the mark of our true identity and goodness and acting from that place. We all take a different journey to discovering our true self. This was mine. I'm not proud of it but I take responsibility for it, all of it. The question is: Would I ever be able to forgive myself for any pain I caused anyone, including David? No one was asking for anything from me. I carried these burdens alone for the most part.

I heard a quote recently that said the only way to be successful was to suffer. I played that role with perfection because I did endure a lot of emotional and mental pain. In my ignorance I was pointing my finger at others as the cause of my suffering, not knowing all the time that I was both the victim and the perpetrator.

Chapter 11

On the Road to Repentance

Amazing grace, How sweet the sound
That saved a wretch like me.
I once was lost, but now I am found,
Was blind, but now I see.
'Twas grace that taught my heart to fear,
And grace my fears relieved.
How precious did that grace appear
The hour I first believed.

~John Newton, Anglican clergyman

The biggest lie in relationships is that two halves make a whole. In a line from the movie *Jerry McGuire*, Tom Cruise's character says to Renee Zellweger's character when trying to get her back, "You complete me." This line could only have been written by a man and it was. His name was Cameron Crowe. Things are progressing, as singer-songwriter Jason Mraz wrote:

> Two halves don't make a whole. Two wholes
> make a whole. In my relationship, I was giving

myself away to make the relationship better, but in actuality, I wasn't doing better by doing that. I became less of a man.

I completely understand what Jason Mraz is saying because that is how I spent most of my life up to the mid-1990s. I was looking for something to complete me and it had to be a man. I wasn't feeling complete in my marriage. I now know that it is always two wholes that create the best and truest relationships. I would find this out but it would be a while before I got there.

I remember seeing this couple who had a deep spiritual relationship. I was somewhat envious, wishing I could have that with David. In the depth of my soul, though we had what we considered to be a good relationship, there was always something missing. We had fun, even with all that craziness we went through with our ménage à trois experimental stage, but I recall some of the times when David and I took walks and he would be talking about how to design or renovate our next house, my mind would always be elsewhere. I would be thinking about some book I'd read on metaphysics or some New Age concept or my next past life regression with Terry.

I believe my spiritual journey started when I left the Catholic Church at sixteen. It doesn't take a church to make us spiritual.

What do I mean by spiritual journey? I am talking about the journey we take into ourselves, really examining our life and trying to connect to something deeper than what we experience in the conditional world. I believe we are all looking for wholeness, to be at peace, to feel our worth, and to fully express who we truly are.

We are not just flesh and bone; we are spiritual beings and every experience we have is a spiritual experience.

Even my rite of passage with my older man and my experimentations in my thirties were part of me trying to find that core of myself, what I now know as my true self; my red dress. At that time my red dress remained fleeting. It was like trying to hold a rainbow in my hand. There is a quote by one of my mentors that goes like this. "We are Spiritual beings, living in a Spiritual universe governed by our use of the Spiritual Law of Cause and Effect." This sums up my journey up to this point. I was governed by *my use* of the Law of Cause and Effect. You wouldn't have been able to tell me that at that time, but in retrospect, it was definitely the truth. There are no victims and all journeys are self-made. Every thought, every belief, every feeling we project into this Universal Law comes back to us in the form of some experience. What we project out into the world regarding how we feel about ourselves comes back to teach us if we are willing to learn. It doesn't mean that others are not responsible for their part in our journey; it just means that we are responsible for our part. I don't want to be a victim. I want to take responsibility for what occurs in my life. It is the only way I can make changes. Life's experiences might take the physical form of pain or joy or being totally lost in the world, but those are just effects. Everything is spiritual. Everything begins in the unseen, as energy, the invisible world beyond what we can see in the three-dimensional world. It is what is called "metaphysical," or beyond the physical. We are all thoughts and beliefs creating experiences, either consciously or unconsciously.

My post ménage à trois spiritual journey began to deepen when I read and completed the work in *The Artist's Way* by Julia Cameron. This coincided with my past life regressions. Then one day I was drawn to have a tarot card reading. The reader told me I would more than likely have more than one marriage. I resisted this idea. I believed I was happily married and refused to think of it in any other way.

On a side note, here's what I feel about tarot cards and psychism. It is very relevant to our life because the psychic is reading our subjective field or subconscious. Our subconscious contains everything that has ever happened to us and everything we are thinking. Most psychics are very gifted in this ability to read our subconscious and that's how they know so much about us. However, a good psychic will always tell you that the cards just suggest and do not compel. In other words, just because something is in the subjective field or subconscious doesn't mean it will happen. It is just a tendency given what you believe and the choices you have made up to that point. I might have been denying that my marriage could possibly end but I also know that I was very unhappy with my life. If I continued down this road, it would end.

In all instances in our lives we can change the trend of causation any time we decide to do so. I apparently had not decided, nor did I want to, and what occurred after this brought the final curtain on my marriage.

One day very soon I would find myself in a heap of tears on the floor of our $180,000, 1995 New Mexico home. Something wasn't right but I wouldn't admit what it was. Instead, I pretended I didn't know. Have you ever done that? You have questions that need answering but you just keep saying, "I don't know."

For me, this is a form of procrastination. When we don't want to make a decision, we just pretend we don't know. At that time in my life, I wasn't willing to do anything different. I just stayed unhappy and looked for solutions in all the wrong places. I know now that the only way to truly change is to be willing to think differently and then do something differently. I could never imagine leaving my twenty-five-year marriage. I believed I loved my husband, and honestly in my own way, I did. There is a quote I heard recently that says, "If you want massive change in your life, you must take massive action."

I would eventually do just that, and the massive change naturally followed.

I had a Master's degree and a teaching job in a prestigious private school that paid me $23,000 a year. After getting one stellar review after another and producing excellent youth theater there, I asked for a raise and was denied. I left that job thinking I was unhappy with what I was doing and upset at being denied the raise. However, that wasn't the reason I left. I walked away to continue my search for meaning. It wouldn't be until a few years later that I'd realize it wasn't my job that was dissatisfying me; it was my life.

To David's dismay, I left without a plan. I don't blame him for being upset. I was expected to contribute to the family income. At the same time, I did my best to be a good mother while dealing with difficult teenagers. One of my daughters had already left home to live with her boyfriend. My other daughter was about to be married in secret because she knew we didn't approve of the boy with whom she was involved. My son would be going to college soon. I'm sure the pull from their social circle contrasted with what we were trying to instill in them regarding college and growing up. They were exploring and we were trying our best to help them while keeping a strong family unit.

In retrospect, I wish I knew what I know now. I could have explained so much more and given so much more guidance than just encouraging them to get an education. David and I were always in disagreement with how we should bring our kids up. I encouraged their dreams and he was the practical one. In reality, it was a good balance and as it turned out, they are all wonderful people. My daughters both have good relationships with the men they have chosen. My son is a stellar father and is on his way to expanding his life after releasing himself from a very difficult and dark relationship.

After leaving my job at the private school, I ran off to Los Angeles at the invitation of an upcoming filmmaker (who I'll call Mike) and the push from my college professor who said this would be a good move for my writing career. One of the things I embarked upon was screenwriting. It was a form of therapy for me as I could get lost in writing fictional stories. At that point my screenwriting partner and I had four or five screenplays under our belt. Mike said he would get me and my scripts into Hollywood. I believed him and left my home and teenagers for six weeks. I remember driving down the driveway and my youngest daughter screaming after me, "Make a lot of money, Mom!" I was sent with David's blessing and the same decree.

What was I looking for that drove me away from my safe home and my duties as Mom? I do not think it was to make a lot of money. Well, that might have been the exterior motive. I would sell a script. I could finally show David I was worth something in the financial world. Up to this point, I continued to be the tax deduction that guaranteed a refund.

My stay in Los Angeles was one of the most difficult six weeks in my life. I didn't know how to be in LA. I was hired as a production assistant, using my own car, my own gas, my own money—and a Thomas Guide (paper map) to find my way on production errands. One day Mike had a meeting with a very famous Hollywood producer. I picked up Mike in my 1990 Camry, dressed in my best outfit—a New Mexico peasant style dress and a pair of sandals. I didn't have a Los Angeles wardrobe nor did I know what it was. I gave it my New Mexico best. I had been instructed by Mike to just sit quietly. "Silence is Power!" he told me. Mike never introduced me to the producer and I did exactly as he told me. I just sat quietly while they spoke.

Once again, I'm not sure what possessed me during that time in my life. I was definitely not living consciously nor did I truly think things through. I believe it was my intense desire to escape from something that I was unconscious of at the time. I disguised my search for meaning with my desire to express myself creatively. I did so in an insane way. As I look back on this drastic choice I made to go to Hollywood, I can see I was only trying to find that red dress of wholeness.

The mythologist and writer, Joseph Campbell, brought the world *The Hero's Journey* which emphasizes three stages: "separation (sometimes called departure), initiation, and return." I had definitely separated from my world as mother and wife and was experiencing some sort of intense initiation. All my insecurities were surfacing and I was slaying them one after another. Would I break into the Hollywood scene and return with some sign of success? That was yet to be known.

Every spiritual journey goes through this maze of confusion until one makes a decision. David came to visit me several times and each time I found myself in the emergency room with a bladder infection. According to Louise Hay, author of *You Can Heal Your Life*, anything to do with the urinary tract coincides with being "pissed off," literally. What was I pissed off at? Who was I pissed off at? I was miserable. I remember crying to my girlfriend on the lobby phone in my apartment building every night. (We didn't have cell phones in those days). She just kept saying, "Why don't you leave and go home?" I just couldn't. I had to do what I came for—to prove my worth. I needed to become something, to make money, to find myself.

Once during my time in Los Angeles, an older Asian man who was the Executive Producer of the film I was working on, invited me to his apartment, claiming he was interested in my screenwriting. He didn't speak a word of English but communicated with me through his translator. I was excited by the prospects of this invitation. Would I make it in Hollywood after all? Suddenly I got a strange gut feeling about the whole thing. I didn't know what it was but it most definitely didn't feel good. I didn't know about intuition in those days. I just convinced myself that I wasn't comfortable accepting this invitation. Honestly, there was a sexual overtone to the whole thing. It wasn't spoken but it was most definitely in the air. I canceled the meeting. Afterwards, the man showed his disdain by never talking to me again. I guess my discomfort was right. It wasn't my screenwriting he was interested in.

During those six weeks in Tinseltown, I found myself emotionally attracted to Mike. We had great conversations. I could talk to him and he could talk to me. He confided in me and told me about his unhappy marriage. Fortunately, nothing sexual came of our relationship. Instead, it just ended abruptly. He was a very volatile person, and one day, he just exploded and told me to get out. Anyone who knows me knows what a hard worker I am so it had nothing to do with my efficiency.

I later found out that the film had crashed. The whole trip was turning into the Titanic. Once the film died, there was no reason for me to be there. My brother, an editor, had just arrived to soak up the Los Angeles vibe. I abruptly left him in my apartment with a mattress that he would be responsible for disposing of. There was a week left on my lease but I just wanted to go home. I couldn't get out of Los Angeles fast enough. I apologized to my brother and came home in what felt like disgrace. I had failed once again. As I entered my home state, the rain began to pound on my car. It was as if the soot of Los Angeles was both literally and metaphorically washing away from me. I drove through the night to get home. I remember collapsing on my king-sized waterbed in complete relief. I felt so safe and secure and happy to be home.

I was in the "return" stage of my hero's journey but I hadn't seemed to bring anything home with me besides shame and failure. For a long time I couldn't figure out what that trip was about. Nothing came of it professionally speaking and I was too immature spiritually to recognize my journey as anything but defeat. As I think it over now, I can only say that I was desperate for something and it had nothing to do with conquering Hollywood or making money. Now I know I was experiencing what we call in the New Thought philosophy, the "Divine Urge."

> The inner desire to express life. The desire to do and accomplish more, to be more completely happy, prosperous and well. It is part of that eternally progressive spirit of unfoldment, and we should surrender the entire situation to the working of Intelligence, with the conviction that Intelligence will use us as a perfect channel.
>
> ~Ernest Holmes, Science of Mind, page 586

I didn't know any of this at that time. If I had, I might have hastened what was to happen next. Instead, I kept denying my true feelings and relegating them to, "I don't know!!! I'm just unhappy!" Why? The answer to that question would not come for a while. Another thing about this inner desire of life to express itself is that when we bury it, it tends to show up in negative behavior. This explains some of my behavior.

I returned home unemployed with no job prospects. I remember taking on motherhood as if I was making my absence up to my kids. I cooked big breakfasts every morning and embraced my housewife life of cleaning, cooking, and more with a new zeal. However, in our family, that wasn't enough. I was supposed to add to the income of the family. I remember being terrified as I fell asleep at night, wondering how I would contribute financially. Out of desperation, I took a job at the New Mexico State Fair. Can you imagine...a talented, educated woman with a Master's degree serving raspberries and ice cream for five dollars an hour? I was relieved to have any job, even that one.

I needed to find better employment but I didn't want to go back to teaching. It was in that moment David and I had an idea. I'm not sure where the idea came from or who came up with it first. We would start a sex catalog business. It was called *Enchanted Creations*. We'd sell sex toys, fantasy cards I'd created, and soft porn. In fact, we found a company that made porn just for women. I was using my creativity but in my most bizarre way so far. In my fairytale fashion, I tried my best to make sex toys into a romantic endeavor. I created a catalog that mimicked the Arthurian age. I even nicknamed myself Guinevere. This did not seem right in my gut but I forged ahead with it anyway. Anything but return-ing to teaching. My aversion to teaching was that it would be all-consuming. I wanted to perform as an actress. I wanted to write. I wanted to be independent and not be a slave to an employer. Our catalog was a poor answer to this but I pursued it anyway, "hoping" to be financially successful.

At one point, David and I went to Vegas for a sex expo to get a better look at this business. I was amazed at the people there. They were normal businessmen and women. There was nothing sleazy about it. However, I felt sleazy. I kept asking myself, "How did I end up here?" I was a performer, an actress, and an amazing singer with an education in the arts and teaching. I remember visiting with one of my college professors who was also a good friend. Of course, we never talked about our sex business. It was shrouded in sexual secrecy and some shame on my part. I don't know how he knew. I guess word does get around. He never criticized me for what I was choosing to do with my life but I know he didn't approve. He was coming to the end of his life. I remember him looking me in the eyes and saying, "A door is opening for you. You must take it." This comment came seemingly out of nowhere. I have this belief that when people are near death, if we are open to listening, they make statements of truth to us from what I believe is the higher realm. At the time I didn't have any idea what door he was referring to but I'll always remember his words.

I finally ended the sex catalog business after a year and a half. I couldn't reconcile my romantic ideal about making love with selling sex toys. I felt cheap and really dirty. I remember sitting on the phone with clients who ordered items. I didn't know it at the time but they were using my verbal product descriptions to sexually excite themselves. I finally got it. After it was all said and done, although in a large part David was the brains behind the operation, I went down in the history of my family as the chief executive officer. Again David said, "I did it for Rita." Interestingly, would you believe we got audited twice during that time? I think the IRS couldn't believe we weren't making hundreds of thousands of dollars instead of the meager $15,000 a year that we earned.

I spun around aimlessly for another couple of years, writing screenplays, taking odd jobs, and raising my teenagers. I had given up on wanting more but there was an undercurrent of something new brewing. I continued settling into my role of the wife who let the man make all the choices. We'd take walks at night, looking at all the homes on our street and David would discuss all the ways he wanted to improve our house and create a life of selling and buying real estate.

Fortunately, I went back to theater for a brief moment. After doing the role of Golde in a huge production of *Fiddler on the Roof*, I again gave up theater, singing, and pretty much everything. I returned to mothering and taking care of our home. Theater was just too time-consuming and my kids needed me during the last few teenage years.

After a couple of years, my kids began moving out of the house. David helped me land a job working for a group of facility managers at the different industrial companies in Albuquerque— Intel, Honeywell, and others. I loved this job. I got to be the organizer, the networker, and I was working with men with whom I felt most comfortable. One of my favorite experiences was arranging the golf tournaments. I was really good at this job and well-loved by all these wonderful men. There was nothing sexual about it yet I felt sexy doing it. It was a time when I accepted myself as a sensual woman with brains. I was most definitely blazing in my red dress. The men depended on me to grow that company, and I did. We went from a half-dozen companies to seventy-five by the time I left that job. It was a time I felt truly fulfilled and happy, at least on the surface. But I still had that longing, that urge for more, and I continued to butt up against that feeling of inferiority and needing to be more than enough. I realize it was this that drove me into overachieving at my job with the facility managers, running the sex business, my trip to Los Angeles, and all those illicit affairs. It motivated me to do more than was expected of me in each of these instances. As I now know more about "wave collapse" in quantum theory, I can see from the scientific standpoint what was creating the feelings I had in all my relationships and experiences.

> Ordinarily, even a single yet significant experience is sufficient to collapse our personal wave of potential. Sometimes all it takes is a hurtful statement or an embarrassing experience in our early years to reduce the potential of our personality to a narrow, restricted self-image. These events need not be traumatic. They may in fact, be subtle. Yet, in those moments our potential fades. It's as if we have taken a snapshot of ourselves and we become frozen in time. I refer to these as confining wave collapses, in contrast to the defining wave collapse that usher in defining moments. We are no longer the potential of the wave but the finiteness of

the particle. And we carry this picture of ourselves with us through our lives, allowing it to burden and limit us. We lose the authorship of our life.

~Mel Schwartz, from The Possibility Principle

I believe in the discoveries of quantum mechanics. I didn't know about it at that time but now I can see how this idea of the wave collapse had limited my life and my self-image. If you think about wave collapse as forming a belief about ourselves that gets wired into our brain, it might make more sense. It happens when someone says the most insignificant or significant thing to you as a child and you believe it. Then you just keep showing up as that, looking for ways to prove it to yourself. Up to that point, my life was a perfect example of this. However, I was about to shift and change. It was finally coming but not in the way I could ever have expected.

Part III - I Am Awake

To be awake is to be alive. ~Henry David Thoreau

Chapter 12

Comet Hale-Bopp, Patrick, and Me

Yours is the light by which my spirit's born. –
Yours is the darkness of my soul's return –
You are my sun, my moon, and all my stars.
~E.E. Cummings

Comet Hale-Bopp was an unusually bright comet that flew by Earth, reaching its closest approach to the planet in 1997. It was most spectacular in the Northern Hemisphere and visible to the naked eye for about eighteen months. Heaven's Gate cult in San Diego committed mass suicide as the comet came close to Earth. ~www.space.com

Heaven's Gate was an end-times cult led by Marshall Applewhite, a former music professor who advocated sexual abstinence and who had undergone castration. Members of the cult

believed that their bodies were merely contain-
ers that could be abandoned in favor of a higher
physical existence. They also thought that an
alien spacecraft was following Hale-Bopp. In
late March 1997, Applewhite and thirty-eight
followers drank a lethal cocktail of phenobar-
bital and vodka and lay down to die, convinced
that they would leave their physical bodies,
enter the alien spacecraft they believed was
behind Hale-Bopp, and pass through Heav-
en's Gate into a higher existence. The bodies of twenty-one women and eighteen men
were found lying in bunk beds in a mansion
in suburban San Diego, California. They wore
matching clothes and new sneakers. According
to material the group posted on its internet
site, the timing of the suicides was probably
related to the arrival of the Hale-Bopp comet
which members seemed to regard as a cosmic
emissary beckoning them to another world.
~*The New York Times*, March 1997

The Hale-Bopp comet suicide was one of those horri-
fying tragic events that touched all of us. Why am I
bringing up the Hale-Bopp comet now? Because I believe
in metaphors and synchronicities. As the Hale-Bopp comet
neared planet Earth and the Heaven's Gate cult chose to take
their lives, I was about to go through the coming of light

into my life and the death of the life I knew for twenty-seven years.

My daughters were all out of the house and my son was ready to go to college to study acting. It was his passion and I especially supported him in fulfilling this dream. As he was deciding whether to become an actor, I thought it would be good for him to acquaint himself with film acting. It came to my attention that there was a film acting and networking studio within the Albuquerque city limits. The studio was called *Feren Studios/Unlimited Productions*. The teacher focused on film acting and networking as an actor in Hollywood. I made the call to the studio on behalf of my son and left for a twenty-five-year anniversary vacation with David. Patrick Feren returned my call while I was away on what I did not know would be the last vacation with my husband. My daughter answered the phone. She told Patrick I was out of town and promised him she'd let me know he had returned my call. This was the simple beginning to what would turn into a massive change in my life.

I was about to return the call when my son let me know he was not really interested in film acting. He never pursued the offer for those classes at *Feren Studios*. I approached David and let him know that I had decided to take the classes instead. I do not believe I had any intention of starting a film career but I needed an outlet for my creativity. What I know about my love for theater and acting is that it always brings about a change in my life. Those times when I have been lured back into its embrace, something was most definitely afoot. This was one of those times.

Soon I met face-to-face with the amazing teacher, Patrick Feren, who brought the actor out in me in a new way. He was the type of teacher who focused on the person's strengths through positive direction, unlike the theatrical training I had received in college which focused on bringing out your best through criticism. Even with a cigarette dangling out of his mouth, Patrick was the most charismatic person I'd ever met.

I felt alive again and fully in my creativity. I distinctly remember when I took my first job as an extra in a film in Santa Fe. Early in the morning before the sun came up, I was driving through the beautiful New Mexico landscape by myself. Tears came to my eyes. Later that day I wrote in my journal that I felt alive again. Was I falling in love? I did not identify it as that.

Patrick always tells the story about our beginnings like this, "I had two rules in my studio. One was everyone always paid on time. Rita always did that. The other is that I would never date a student." The truth is Patrick and I never planned to date each other or become lovers. A short time into my affiliation with the studio, I began to work for him in exchange for classes. It was a win/win relationship for which I will always be grateful. Our relationship started as strictly professional. I respected him as the leader of his studio and as my teacher. Underneath all of this, something else was definitely happening. Our professional relationship quickly grew into a friendship. Even now, I know this element has always strengthened our bond. When couples begin as friends, I believe their relationship has a solid anchor. Ours did and that friendship has held true for over twenty-seven years now.

At that time, I knew nothing about the Law of Cause and Effect. I wasn't even thinking about how I had focused on having a spiritual partner several years ago when I witnessed that couple who were so spiritually connected. I didn't know that while I had worked on my own spirituality these last few years, I was also preparing myself for a spiritual partner to come into my life. That is the way the Law of Cause and Effect works. It's called "embodiment." Spirit creates by becoming the thing it desires. I had immersed myself in my spiritual growth through the New Age movement. As I became my own spiritual partner, it was no coincidence that my mirror would show up in my life. What would I do about it? Now that was a different story, as we are always at choice.

There was a kismet quality to my relationship with Patrick as if our first meeting was destined. I do not believe in kismet. I believe we create our own destiny. When we are ready for change, change shows up. We are always at choice. I had encountered Patrick many months before. We met at an acting workshop held by an Albuquerque casting director. I remember seeing him across a crowded room with his long hair, cowboy boots, and that dangling cigarette, knowing intuitively that I would get to know him some day. I remember saying to myself, "I'm going to know that guy." As I have been learning in quantum theory, time is fluid and there is no past or future. Right now is all there is. When I saw Patrick across that room and then made that statement with such clarity, was I collapsing waves of possibility in the unified field, concretizing that eventual meeting? I believe

I was. We were like two parts of one particle on opposite sides of the Universe, always connected and bound to unite again in the physical. It sure explains why I wrote several screenplays that mirrored Patrick's life before I ever met him. They had aspects of Patrick's life in them that I could never have known about. Here is a beautiful quote to which I resonate.

> When you separate an entwined particle and you move both parts away from the other, even at opposite ends of the universe, if you alter or affect one, the other will be identically altered or affected. Spooky. ~Adam in *Only Lovers Left Alive*, Jim Jarmusch

There is no destiny projected upon us. We are always at choice and in charge of our own fate. I will say there was a higher knowing within me that urged me to leap into this experience with Patrick and *Feren Studios* before the opportunity passed me by. Looking back, I believe that the door that my mentor spoke of several months before was finally opening. I consciously jumped in. I never thought about the other two relationships that had ended in disaster. This was different in my mind. It was a very deep friendship and connection. I do not think either of us really knew how deep.

Patrick and I were spending a lot of time together because when it comes to work, I give my all. I was totally committed to acting, working in his studio, and finally realizing that my career as an actress that I had shoved aside might actually happen. When I told my father about this new teacher in my life, I remember his exact words, "This man will change your life, finally." Patrick certainly changed my life but I'm sure it wasn't in the way my father envisioned.

David and I decided to have Patrick to dinner at our house. My father continued to coach me and let me know I should cook a very special meal for Patrick to impress him. Food and its importance in life was a big part of my father's consciousness. It was the logical place for my father to start in trying to solidify our relationship which he seemed bent upon doing. You would have thought he was setting me up for a marriage possibility. My father also knew Patrick was connected to the entertainment industry and my father still had that vision for me. Is it possible for our higher selves to know something that isn't consciously known to us? Yes, I believe it is. Otherwise, how would our evolution always find ways to bring us back to ourselves? When I say "ourselves," I am talking about our true selves, our soul's purpose, the reason we are here on Earth. Even challenges are the higher consciousness within us calling us home.

What would have driven my father to make sure this relationship with Patrick was secured, outside of him envisioning a dream for me as an entertainer? I insist that on some plane of action, there was more happening and my father was an integral part of it. Several years later, when I married Patrick and my father was gone from this Earth, I remember a vivid dream. My family was all present in the dream, even Grandma Hertz who had also passed away many years before. It was very real. Everyone was smiling and approving of my marriage to Patrick, including my father. That seems impossible since my father was Catholic and divorce was a no-no. But this dream was so real and filled with approval. I will never forget it. The only person who had a look of disdain on her face was my Aunt Lucile. This made total sense to me because my aunt liked David so much. Although she supported me in my marriage to Patrick, I never felt that she totally approved. However, her love for me superseded any judgment she might have felt.

The first night Patrick came to dinner, we had a wonderful evening, talking, and getting to know each other. Later after Patrick had left, David used that favorite phrase of his that led to those three-way trysts we previously experienced, "I can tell you like him." Well, of course I liked him but I had no intention of going back to the past and the emotional disasters that followed. This was a friendship and a professional relationship and that is what I intended for it. But David wasn't wrong either. As my professional relationship and friendship with Patrick grew, even if I was denying it, something deeper was arising within me. It wasn't sexual at first but it was a longing to meet in the mind. It was a spiritual connection; his spiritual beliefs and mine coincided on all levels. It was a bond that went beyond acting or working together. As we began to know each other more deeply, our love for acting would be the container that would hold us.

So much was coming together for me theatrically, including my writing. I was excited when Patrick was willing to do readings of my screenplays at his studio. There was one particular script I had written after my last disastrous ménage à trois relationship. It was called *Breaking All the Rules*. When I wrote this script with David and my writing partner at the time, I wrote it with the intention of exploring what it would be like if a ménage à trois were to work out. It was healing for me and one of the only scripts I ever wrote that would eventually go into development. I gave Patrick the script to read in hopes that we could do a reading at the studio. I remember that I was hesitant before giving it to him. I thought, what's he going to think? Will he think I'm suggesting that three-way relationships are okay? Would it make him feel uncomfortable? I didn't hear back from him and I was too polite to push him.

Here is another moment of truth about time and space being fluid. The script did eventually get read in Patrick's studio. Much later, discussing his hesitancy to read the script and the length of time it took him to get back to me, Patrick told me it was because he was afraid to read it. He had no logical reason for putting it off. He didn't even know what it was about. He said he would look at it on the floor by his bed and just push his desire to read it away. When I asked him what he was afraid of, he said he feared if he read it, it would come true. His intuition was correct because the story played itself out before our very eyes. It wasn't until much later that we realized we were in the middle of that screenplay, unfolding as our life.

Now as a spiritual leader, I use this story in my talks as an example of how to make a demonstration. It might have been somewhat unconscious in that I didn't know the power of what I was doing, but I had visualized and written the details of something I apparently wanted deeply. It was about healing for me. At the time I had no idea that I was doing what we call in Dr. Joe Dispenza's work, "meeting my future self." I was actually visualizing something I wanted with an intensity of feeling, sending that intention out into the Universe. It was the intense feeling that would bring the story back to me as my life. Recently I was listening to Barbra Streisand's autobiography, *My Name is Barbra*. She tells the story of how she met James Brolin at the same time she was completing the film *The Mirror Has Two Faces*. She had made a decision that she would finally produce a film in which she got the guy. And in real life, she did. I don't think we have to write a full-length script or produce a movie to manifest our dreams, but we do have to continue to visualize those dreams with feeling and then take massive action.

The day came when David finally invited Patrick to go more deeply and intimately into our relationship. Patrick didn't agree at first. There were several weeks of resistance on his part including the possibility of an ending to our relationship altogether. I'm sure he had a lot to think about since he later told me he thought David and I had a perfect relationship, idyllic really. He was in total confusion. In addition to this, he was at a period in his life when he was single and comfortable. He was immersed in creating his studio and I'm certain he didn't want any distractions, especially something as intense as this had the promise to be.

The three of us kept getting together for social engagements—movies, theater, meals, etc. Patrick and I continued to work at the studio. At the same time, I was still working for the facility managers and enjoying that. Patrick, David, and I were becoming very close. Our conversations were deep and stimulating.

Finally, one night it happened. We consummated our relationship but not in the same way as the other three-way relationships. It evolved suddenly and unexpectantly. I would not be a sexual object between two men. David would not be a voyeur. It was Patrick who insisted on all three of us being in the bed together, no holds barred, so to speak. We knew everything about each other at this point, including that Patrick considered himself to be bisexual. As I write this, I am a bit nervous to be so honest, but I want to tell the truth in this book and I have Patrick's permission to do so.

This shift in our relationship with Patrick was the beginning of me finally and truly finding my red dress. It was a surprise to me but David actually seemed anxious to sexually engage with Patrick. I was also surprised that I didn't mind and felt it was sexy. As I embarked on this new exploration, I did not know that this first night of consummating our relationship was also the beginning of the end of my marriage to David.

I was undoubtedly falling in love with Patrick and it went far beyond a sexual attraction. Interestingly, I was never jealous of David's relationship with Patrick. In fact, I encouraged it because I felt if that could be solidified, I wouldn't lose Patrick. It was Patrick that I wanted but not because of the sex. There was so much more in store for us. I didn't understand any of it at that time. I was just a woman still exploring and wondering and searching for that something that would bring me wholeness. I would eventually find that with Patrick, not because he completed me, but because I could stand alone beside him. I would finally understand what it meant to become "two wholes making a whole."

It isn't easy for me to be so honest and transparent here. In fact, as I began writing this book, I had to pretend that I would never publish it. I did this because I wanted the words to spill onto the page from a totally authentic and vulnerable place. Truthfully, I had never been in bed with any man up to this point where I felt just fine and whole whether he returned my love or not. I remember thinking to myself, "This is what unconditional love is all about." I never obsessively pursued Patrick nor did I act weak or needy. I didn't look for approval. I didn't care if I was accepted. I just simply loved him for who he was. I loved the way we worked together. I loved the way we created together. I loved the way we dreamed together. He could do whatever he wanted to do with David if it would keep us together.

However, Patrick never really wanted David. Patrick is a bisexual male and that made it okay with him to engage sexually with David. Later, he admitted that he was never physically attracted to David. As Patrick looked back on everything that transpired, he confided in me that he believes what he was doing was purposefully taking me out of the role of whore. He might not have known this at the time, but do we always know the internal side of our objectives in life? There are mysteries that do not reveal themselves until later. Patrick does admit that he eventually grew to love David. What wasn't there to love? David was a kind and generous man and a lot of fun too.

So, how did it all play out? Our relationship was idyllic and magical for one year. We did everything together. We would go to the theater in our community and we would always be asked if the reservation was for three. People knew but it remained unspoken. My grown children even knew about our relationship and accepted it.

Some of those magical times included a camping trip. As it is with many of us who are entrepreneurs, it was hard to drag Patrick away from his studio. One weekend he agreed to go camping with us. I remember when we picked him up. He was standing outside of his studio in that denim shirt I had so often seen him in. He had cut off the sleeves. He later told me he'd cut them off as a metaphorical statement of freedom. That camping trip was just that—a weekend of freedom in the wild. One of the things I remember was waking up in the middle of the night to the sound of loud mooing. We peered out of our tent window to find a group of cattle surrounding our tent, just staring at us in the moonlight. I will always remember the one cow with the long antlers. We were kind of spooked and wondered if they were aliens. We were outside of Roswell, New Mexico, so who knows. Anything was possible and everything seemed possible. It was a crazy and wonderful time.

The one and only time we celebrated Christmas together, Patrick had planned to spend the holidays with his mom in the Bay Area. We moved our celebration to the week before Christmas. Our grown children were out of the house at that time. The celebration was magical, like a fairytale. It was snowing and we spent three days together, making love, eating, opening presents, and playing like children.

During that blissful year, we thought our three-way affair could be lasting. David was so invested in this relationship that he brought it not only to our children's attention, but to his own parents' attention. He insisted on being honest with everyone. In fact, he was about to add Patrick to the will and made an appointment with a financial advisor. I remember the look on that advisor's face. He said nothing but he proceeded to help us to change our financial affairs. The only person who didn't know was Patrick's mom. I think she suspected but she never confronted Patrick and he didn't tell her. I remember her saying to others, "They are very close."

After that first perfect year, things began to turn toward a very dramatic ending. The screenplay I had written seemed to pave the way to the final curtain on the very last three-way relationship I would ever experience, and to the ending of my marriage to David. It started when David sent Patrick and me off to Los Angeles. The screenplay *Breaking All the Rules* was in development. At the same time, Patrick and I had a cabaret act that was getting some attention in Albuquerque. Then there was my desire to begin my acting career in Los Angeles. I had reached the heights and depths of what I could do in Albuquerque. Could I make it in Los Angeles? With Patrick at my side, I knew anything was possible. David was sure we would be successful and promised to join us as soon as he retired which could be as soon as two years. In the meantime, he came for fun on the weekends.

Then suddenly, a few months after our move, David let us know he couldn't make the change nor could he leave his job. He didn't feel retiring was an option for him because things had changed at his company. They moved his retirement a few more years into the future. He wasn't willing to lose his retirement by trusting in something that might or might not prove financially successful—Patrick's or my career. I never blamed David for wanting this security. From the day we were married, monetary security was of utmost importance to him. I, on the other hand, was so trusting and living in the moment. I always had the idea, and still do, that things will always work out. David was a pros and cons man. That's how we lived much of our life together. This situation, for him, weighed heavily on the "con" side.

Why couldn't we just continue as we were with David visiting a couple of times a month and Patrick and I working toward our careers? At first, we all honestly thought it would work. In the meantime, as Patrick and I went through the ups and downs of our daily lives in Los Angeles together, we grew closer and closer. David wasn't part of those struggles and joys and it was hard to share that intimacy with someone who was becoming more and more of an outsider to our day-to-day experiences. When David came in on weekends, it seemed to be focused on the physical aspects of our relationship without the emotional intimacy. Compounding this was that during the in-between times, Patrick and I were making love without David. Also, there was a spiritual aspect that we couldn't share with David. Patrick and I had a deep spiritual intimacy and that was separating us from David. I remember a Christmas Eve close to the end when we took Patrick's mom to midnight mass. Patrick and I were fine with this and enjoyed the Catholic ritual. David was so bored that he fell asleep.

I was also introduced to the Science of Mind at that same time. As a result, David was even more emotionally separated from us. Finally, I could no longer live the lie. I had fallen out of love with David and was totally committed and in love with Patrick. In retrospect, I can see that it was perfectly orchestrated by David, even if it was unconscious. Moving on could never have included David. As we had already proven to each other throughout the years of our marriage, we wanted different things. Now we were finally able to admit it. David was ready to move on and get back to what he had always wanted—security. I never gave him that, and even though he loved my adventurous spirit, he was so much happier in the material world without me. I am not lessening the pain we both felt in the ending of our relationship. As I made this choice, it was as if I took the life line on my palm and yanked it in another direction. However, I know it was totally right. The ending had come.

Naturally, David would tell everyone that he did it for me and that *I* left *him,* but I can tell you that the divorce papers came through the fax machine on December 31, one day after we decided on a divorce. That's not possible unless it was planned that way. As time went on, in my children's eyes, I became the one who left their father. Everyone seemed to have forgotten the relationship that we openly and honestly shared with all of them and the changing of the will. It would take several years to heal these wounds. Again, I found myself stuck in the role of the bad one who brought pain and sorrow to everyone. This time it would be different and I would heal. I had found the Science of Mind that would take me through a completely new passage to wholeness.

Chapter 13

My Life Is Unfolding Perfectly

Every perfect life is a parable invented by God.
~Simone Weil

L et me take a little step back to before the divorce from David. One of the beliefs I have, after many years of practicing the Science of Mind and Spirit, is that "my life is unfolding perfectly." This means that no matter what is occurring, whether I am conscious of it or whether I am living in the 95 percent of my mind that is my subconscious, my life is and always will be unfolding perfectly. This is not because there is a destiny for me, but because the Divine in me, that higher Intelligence, is always bringing me back to Itself. When I get off course, I am never really lost. I'm just evolving in the way that I am consciously capable of in that moment. Wherever I am in consciousness, there I am in life. My life is a perfect reflection or mirror of my conscious awareness.

As Patrick and I took off that day for Los Angeles with David's encouragement "to get our careers going," I know that my life was unfolding perfectly. As we entered LA on the

101-freeway driving north, I will never forget us in that little red car wedged in the center of what seemed like hundreds of semi-trucks. I was definitely in the unknown, but totally excited and expectant of a new and amazing life. I was in love, not just with Patrick, but with this new life I had chosen for myself. I was conscious for the first time. I knew in the heart of me that this was right. My kids were grown. My youngest was married. My other daughter was living with her boyfriend and my son was in New York trying to make it as an actor.

Is it possible that on some level you know your future and what is to come? Yes! As I said, time is fluid in the now moment. I remember a specific thought I had when we decided to have our children so young— one, two, three—twenty-two months apart. At the time I thought to myself, I'm having children young and close together so that after parenthood, I can have another life and not be too old to enjoy it. I didn't know what that life would be but something within me knew it was the road I should take. You see, my life was unfolding perfectly and my higher self was guiding me all the time. This is the same truth for all of us. Wouldn't it be wonderful if we could trust that and make our choices accordingly? And even when we don't, things come back around. I remember a day long before this and way before I ever met Patrick when I was making the decision between choosing acting as my major or pursuing a degree in education. I was walking on the UNM campus and remember feeling that sinking feeling when I went against what I truly felt in my heart. I chose security over the passion I had for theater. So as I began this new section of my life in Los

Angeles, I can see that it is never too late to start again or to make another choice. Whenever I talk to people who are grappling with whether to follow their passion or security in their future, I often tell them this story. It's never too late, and if you remain open, your passion will win out.

There I was in Los Angeles ready to take it all on, ready to be an actress, ready to sell my screenplays. If I knew at the time what would become of me, I probably would have cut to the chase and entered ministerial school because that is where I ended up. However, there was more to learn first.

I remember the nights of making love to the sound of the breakdowns coming in on the fax machine at two in the morning. (Breakdowns are the notices that are put out by the producers and casting directors letting actors know what shows and movies are casting). I remember prancing across the studio lawns, dropping off headshots. There once was a time when you could just walk onto a studio lot right into a casting director or producer's office. This was before the tragedy of 9/11.

It was the best of times and the worst of times. Patrick and I had no money. We were in debt. We thought we were having an acting career when we actually spent most of our time auditioning for jobs while being actors in the most creative ways. At one time, Patrick was employed as Santa Claus. We tried to go it alone but finally got hooked into a Santa management company. We paid quite a few bills with that gig. Patrick still gets job offers from that company twenty-three years later. Can you imagine he's still in their database? We smile every time those job offers come in now as we remember the beginnings of our relationship. We were passionate, hardworking, and we would do anything to get our careers rolling.

We both worked as standardized patients almost immediately upon arriving in Los Angeles. A standardized patient is a program used in most medical universities that employs actors to assist doctors in bedside manners and examination skills. What a blessing that job was! Somehow we always had enough to eat and pay our rent.

We produced our own plays when no one would hire us. Actors act, and we didn't let the Hollywood industry's lack of response stifle our creative urge. We even created workshops to get ourselves inspired. I don't think there has been a day in our life together when we weren't creating something. Even now, we wake up to creativity. "What will this day be like? I wonder..." That's how we begin every day and then we do a Spiritual Mind Treatment to solidify our day. (A Spiritual Mind Treatment is an affirmative prayer or a movement of energy in a specific direction following our intention and empowered by our feelings).

It was a romantic time but I would be lying if I said there wasn't a dark side to it all. Patrick and I stayed solid in our relationship but not without guilt on my part. I arrived in Los Angeles in the throes of sciatica, debt, and on the verge of divorce. In other people's eyes, Patrick was my friend and I still had a husband in New Mexico. That is how everyone in Los Angeles knew me at that time. I was living a secret once again.

When I say that my life is unfolding perfectly, I mean that as we are directing our life's course, the Universe assists us with the support required to meet the challenges that occur.

In that unfolding, when we decide that what we really want is to be happy and whole, the Universe provides the path. On my path, I would find the Science of Mind and Spirit and the road to ministry.

Chapter 14

I'm No Angel

I wrote the story myself. It's about a girl who lost
her reputation and never missed it.

~Mae West from the film I'm No Angel

F or what seemed like the first time in a long time, I was
following what we call in the Science of Mind, "the
Divine Urge." I was terrified. I didn't know what the Divine
Urge was. I only knew what I truly wanted for the first time
in my life. I never went back to New Mexico. Even though
everything was saying, "You should," at the same time my
higher self was saying, "Los Angeles is where you belong."

Patrick also realized that he belonged in Los Angeles
where his dream had led him so long ago. It was time to take
on this dream of a full-time acting career, full force. We had
no idea where it would lead us but we began the trek anyway.
As Martin Luther King Jr. once wrote, "Faith is taking the
first step without seeing the whole staircase."

I had been in Los Angeles for less than a month when I was
introduced to my first Science of Mind Church in Burbank.
Rev. Dr. Marlene Morris was the Senior Minister. Patrick
had been trying to get me into a Religious Science Church

back in New Mexico. I wouldn't go because I had sworn off churches after Mormonism. I never thought I'd find myself in another church but there I was. Unbeknownst to me, it was a Divine appointment. When we arrived in LA, Patrick encouraged me to go by telling me I would really enjoy this woman minister who he had seen before. Rev. Dr. Marlene hooked me the moment I went to the first Sunday service. My first impression during the service was that this wasn't a church. At least it didn't seem like one. Our members here on Kaua'i have called our Center "not a church" because the Science of Mind has no dogma. We do not tell people what to do or what to think. We do teach them how to think. What's the difference? Well, learning how to think from a place of love, whether for yourself or for others, will never steer you in the wrong direction. I believe Science of Mind teachers and leaders teach by their own example.

The first service I attended was in the middle of a series of talks Dr. Marlene called *My Heart's Desire.* How perfect for me, a budding, older actress trying to make it in Los Angeles! There are no coincidences. Was she talking just to me from her pulpit? It certainly seemed so. Here I was, forty-five years old, trying to begin a career as an actress in a field that practiced ageism. Could I really have my heart's desire? That first Sunday at the Burbank Church of Religious Science is where I believe my conscious spiritual journey began. My life would slowly begin to turn in another direction, almost against my own human willpower, as I began to align myself with Divine Will. For those who do not know the term "Divine Will," it is not about willpower, nor is it the will of an outside God. In the Science of Mind, it states:

> The Spirit does not have to will to make things
> happen; things happen because it is the will of
> Spirit that they should be. This will, then, is
> simply the execution of a purpose; and since
> Spirit is Absolute, there can be nothing to deny
> its Will. ~*Science of Mind*, page 645

In other words, there is a higher consciousness within each of us that is intuiting through us and leading and guiding our path. Divine Will is that consciousness, and when we align ourselves with it, truly listening to that inner voice, our paths begin to unfold with ease and grace.

Finding the Science of Mind and the term "my heart's desire" was about more than just my acting and screenwriting career. I had found a philosophy that made total sense to both my logic and my deep longing for a God that I didn't even know I missed. From the time I entered that first Science of Mind Church in 1998, I don't think I have missed more than two dozen Sundays. And when I did miss, it was because I was traveling and there wasn't a church in the vicinity.

I found my red dress in the Science of Mind teaching. There was no judgment about the life I'd lived up to this point. It reminds me of a quote by Adrienne Maree Brown. "I touch my own skin, and it tells me that before there was any harm, there was miracle."

In this philosophy I was accepted as Perfection and someone who was on the road of revealing God as herself. In the Science of Mind *Declaration of Principles*, it states: "We believe in our own soul, our own spirit, and our own destiny; for we understand that the life of all is God." There was no outside God to fear or judge me. God was as close as my own breath and in my own heart. I was an expression of Divinity, flaws and all. God is always here, even at the worst times. It is only about revealing God, recognizing ourselves as an expression of God, which expands its presence within us.

In the first month at the Burbank Center, I jumped into spiritual classes. Within a year, I was on my way to becoming a practitioner, while all the time I was still pursuing my acting career. I had a few acting successes but nothing was really happening for me in that arena. As I mentioned earlier, I put a one-woman show together quite successfully. I called that an acting career for a while, and it was. *Tomatoes on a Windowsill* was the story about me growing up under the rule of my Italian father. It was a ministry in itself and I had an incredible time doing it. Patrick directed me and we produced it together. My first run was a fundraiser for our Church. I touched many people as I traveled with this ministry disguised as a theatrical production for over three years.

Tomatoes on a Windowsill is a significant part of my development and the claiming of my red dress. I wrote the script. The play was all about my relationship with my father and his struggle to control me and my fight to resist it. I believe through the writing of this piece and the three years that I toured with it, completing over one hundred performances, that I released some of my shame surrounding my past. As I stood on that stage one hundred times and sang

Ave Maria in my red dress, both in defiance of my father and at the same time, in total acceptance and love for him, I healed my past, one performance at a time. In scientific terms, I literally rewired my brain and reframed my past. I gave my life a different perspective.

Writing and performing *Tomatoes on a Windowsill* also gave me a container to understand and heal my own soul in my relationship with David. I was able to become the observer of the little girl who so wanted to escape the constraints put upon her by her domineering father that she literally ran head on into the arms of another authoritative figure. He was kind and loving and encouraging, but still she transferred her belief in not-enoughness to her relationship, and not just with her husband, but with the other men in her life. I was a child feigning adulthood and doing a good job at it. I believe that is why I spent so much of my life in my thirties trying to relive the teenage life I never had. *Tomatoes on a Windowsill* brought all of this to a moment of clarity as I began to embrace my totality as a woman who was still growing. With Patrick, I finally embraced a partner with whom to continue that journey. (If you would like to view *Tomatoes on a Windowsill*, it is available for free on our YouTube channel: http://tiny.cc/rpxwzz

As I dove deeper into the Burbank Church, I was studying and growing in the teaching of the Science of Mind and Spirit. There was so much in it that brought clarity to my life. It is a teaching that simply says we are responsible for our life. We are always causing effect and living those effects as experiences. What we put out mentally and physically into the world *does* come back to us. What better place than this to finally take responsibility and heal my past? What happened to Patrick and me? We grew together in the Science of Mind and Spirit while still pursuing our acting and film careers. We were married by Rev. Dr. Marlene on July 1 of 2001.

It would soon be time to leave those desires for acting behind. You might wonder why a philosophy that told me I could do, be, and have anything did not catapult me to stardom. Looking back on it now, I see it is because I didn't believe it at the time. I was not ready for it. I was not equal to it. I was so nervous at auditions, I sabotaged myself many times. I think sometimes we think we know what we want but we just don't have the belief system to support it. What I realize is that everything comes down to self-worth and at that time I was still facing my lack of it. I remember one of my mentors telling me that he roomed with a famous actor who may or may not have been especially talented, but he had star mentality. He believed in his ability to become a star and so it is! Belief backed by determination and lots of faith in action breaks down what seems like unsurmountable walls. As the famous filmmaker George Lucas once wrote, "You have to find something that you love enough to be able to take risks, jump over the hurdles and break through the brick walls that are always going to be placed in front of you. If you don't have that kind of feeling for what it is you are doing, you'll stop at the first giant hurdle." That idea is what Patrick and I would apply to building the Center for Spiritual Living Kaua'i. But for right now, I was still building my faith and my ability to leap over unsurmountable walls.

Nothing we do in life is ever lost, and whatever path we follow, it is always taking us back to ourselves. Some of us do that in this life. Some have to transition to do so. If you are not familiar with the term "to transition," it means to die or pass away. We use the term transition because it signifies that someone is moving on to another level of existence. As a minister, I have witnessed people in transition reviewing their lives. Sometimes they are satisfied and sometimes there is still a longing for what they feel they did not accomplish. I always do my best to lead them back to self-love and a sense of peaceful completion. We are never done and I do believe we continue into the next level of existence, always expanding.

For me, I was determined to live as largely as I can in this life. I've always been told I had a resilient spirit. I remember an acting teacher coaching me after I lost the part of my dreams in college. "What I know about you, Rita, is you have the ability to get right back up and start again." This is one of my strengths that carried me through my Los Angeles days.

All through my life I'd always been told I was unfocused, but on my path to ministry, I began to realize that everything I'd ever done from teaching to singing to acting to mothering would come together in one thing, and that one thing would be ministry. However, ministry and Kaua'i were still almost a decade away.

Chapter 15

The Rising Corpse

Human beings, we have dark sides; we have dark issues in our lives. To progress anywhere in life, you have to face your demons.

~John Noble

In many horror or thriller movies, there is something I call "the rising corpse." This aspect of writing is played out well in the last scene of the movie and play *Wait Until Dark*. It happens when you think the villain is dead and then he/she suddenly rises for one last strike at the hero/heroine. I liken this plot twist to my experience overcoming my feelings of not being enough. Although I thought I had dismissed my victimhood, feelings of inferiority, and fear of authority, I would soon invite myself to another dance with authority and I would willingly take my partner by the hand and dance. The difference is that this time, because I was awake, I wouldn't leave the dance until I had completed the steps with confidence.

Patrick and I stayed at the Burbank Church until things there began to move in a different direction. Dr. Marlene became ill and she just couldn't maintain the ministry anymore. In her decline, new leaders were arising and their vision wasn't one we resonated with. It was time for us to move on. We needed a place to expand further.

Leaving a church family is like leaving a real family. I experienced that once before when I left the Mormon Church. In that situation, the Mormons came after us for a couple of years. This would be quite different. It was difficult to let go because of the deep love and admiration we had for Dr. Marlene. The timing of her retirement and our decision to leave was perfect. Unlike my Mormon experience, she let us go with grace and ease. That's what people who love you do, and Dr. Marlene loved Patrick and me very much. One thing I will never forget is her love.

It's interesting to say you left a church for the teaching, but that is what we did. We never gave up the Science of Mind philosophy. To this day, we say if the whole organization were to fall apart, the Science of Mind teaching would still be our life's foundation. It was, and is, the most important thing in our lives. Recently we heard of another part of the organization shutting down. Patrick retorted, "Well, you can't close Ernest Holmes." That is the truth. This great mystic's message will live on even if all the organizations close. It is the teaching, not the organization, that keeps us alive and growing.

Patrick and I continued to grow spiritually and emotionally together. We looked for another center where we could deeply plant our spiritual roots. We checked out every Religious Science Church we could find in Los Angeles while at the same time keeping a low profile. We knew how easy it was for us to jump in and get involved. We wanted the right place this time because we had a specific mission—to finally become Science of Mind Practitioners.

One day, by pure synchronicity via a Los Angeles theater production, we found Rev. Chris and the Center for New Beginnings. Once again, it would be theater that brought me to the place where I would certainly evolve. As soon as we entered the doors, the Center for New Beginnings became our home. To this day it is still the most loving and spiritually enlightening place on the planet for me. I met people there who remain my dear friends, people who are family, and who I know I can call upon for anything. This was family as I'd never understood the word before. Perhaps as we grow in Spirit, our relationships also grow in Spirit. I believe that is true.

So much happened at the Center for New Beginnings. I grew up there, spiritually speaking, and I found what would be yet another release from not-enoughness. It was one of the most exhilarating and the most difficult times in my life. However, remember this: when you make the intention to expand, everything will come up to test the strength of your intention. Rev. Donna Michael, a New Thought minister and songwriter, calls it "the last gasp of a dying fear."

Rev. Chris is a charismatic and powerful leader. He is the embodiment of love and those who work with him eagerly jump in to serve him and his ministry. He is so integrated in the teaching that you want to dive in with him, not only because of his words, but with how he lives his life.

Rev. Chris fully pushed my buttons around my victimhood, authority pleasing, and feeling like I was not enough. I must have been ready for another jump into healing and he provided the path. I served in his ministry from 2006 to 2013. I was loyal, supportive, and active. When he had a vision, I was there to assist him in accomplishing it. I remember once when he talked about having a labyrinth in the building. I immediately took it upon myself to create one. We had a deep connection, and after what I call trial by fire, I became his confidant and friend. He and his husband are the dearest people in my life next to my husband and children.

It wasn't always that way though. This is where the trial by fire comes in. When I started ministerial training with him, there was a shift in our relationship to what felt like the dark side. My shadow self would come forth. My people-pleasing Achilles heel met head on with his authoritative personality. As a ministerial student, he seemed to attack me ferociously. I couldn't do anything right—whether it was giving a talk or doing a Spiritual Mind Treatment. I sat frozen in his class and cried many nights. Now I clearly see it was all part of my development; the way that I would grow up yet again. I would meet my own father as Rev. Chris. I wanted to please him so badly, and when I didn't, things went south for me. I lost all confidence. I became like a little girl again looking up at Daddy and wishing he'd love me. Yikes! I thought I was over this!

After one particularly difficult evening in ministerial class, I was crying so hard that I couldn't drive the car into the garage. Patrick was at a loss and not the most patient with me. Being the inner child expert he is, he saw what was happening. I was blind to it. I was a victim and I made Rev. Chris my perpetrator. I realize now that I was the one who let everything negatively affect me during those early years of our relationship. I let him influence how I felt about my singing, my acting, my ability to write, and so much more.

I often tell people that I started in this Science of Mind philosophy as a victim. It's hard to admit, but it's true. The thing I resisted the most was when Rev. Chris would call me on my victimhood. I'd think, why can't he see that he's abusing me? He's the one that's wrong. I'm not saying he wasn't sometimes cruel in his ability to critique a talk or treatment. I'm just asking myself why I didn't see it all for what it was—me recreating my relationship with my father. I would eventually come to that knowing but there had to be one last battle. After it all was over, and still to this day, Rev. Chris and I remain the best of friends. It happened like this.

I graduated from ministerial school with the highest grade in the national written exam. After passing the exam, a ministerial candidate must go through oral panels and an intensive week of workshops. After five days in Monterey, California filled with workshops and giving talks, the oral panels would be next. I was sure I would fail those panels. I look back now on a woman who was so insecure. Sometimes we worry ourselves about things that will never ever happen. I'd been a worrywart since kindergarten. Here was another great opportunity. I remember Rev. Chris saying to me, "If they don't pass you, I'm leaving Centers for Spiritual Living." He believed in me but it didn't matter. I cried myself to sleep that night. When I awoke the next day, something had changed within me. I knew no matter what this panel decided, I would be a minister. No one could stop me from taking this next step in my life. A day later, I would find out that I passed the oral panels and was granted my ministerial license.

After I graduated, all I wanted to do was be a full-time minister. Nothing else interested me. Patrick and I were still on the same path. We both wanted full-time ministry. Patrick became a part-time paid staff minister with the youth at the Center while I was working as a writer for a children's internet company and volunteering at the Center whenever I could. I volunteered as the head of Pastoral Care and Outreach.

My writing job was a great job with benefits. It got me through ministerial school. However, again it was time for change. My Divine Urge was rising. I hated missing ministerial events because I was working. What would I do? I went to Rev. Chris one day and said, "I'm quitting my job and I want to be your Assistant Minister." He just looked at me. I think I shocked him. Then he said, "I don't see you in that position." He said something else to support his argument. I don't remember what it was but I was devastated. I'd learned not to wear my emotions on my sleeve with him. Instead, I said, "If it's money, I don't care." I threw his own line back at him. "God is the source and substance of my supply." I believed it. I was ready to put my faith into action.

We ended the conversation with him saying he'd think about it. Surprisingly, he came back the next day saying he thought it was a good idea. I'm not sure what changed his mind. At the time I didn't know what I was getting myself into. I just knew I wanted ministry full-time and this was the only way I saw it happening. Little did I know that this would be the most difficult job in my life. We continued to discuss my employment and he said he thought he could come up with $1000 a month part-time salary for me. It was a long way from my present earnings but I took it. I gave notice at my writing job. I'm sure Patrick was nervous about this. Who wouldn't be? It was half of our family income. However, Patrick didn't try to talk me out of it.

What happened next was Divine Intervention. Rev. Chris's administrator suddenly up and quit. There was now an open job as administrator. Of course, I wouldn't take it without the title of Assistant Minister. Rev. Chris said yes. I moved into a job where I was making almost as much as I was in my writing job. I didn't have the same benefits but that was okay. I thought I was finally a full- time minister. I could do what I loved all day long. I would also learn how to run a church from the inside out. I know I was one of the best things that happened to Rev. Chris. I was loyal. I worked hard and joyfully. I didn't count my hours. I gave everything. At times, Patrick and I butted heads about it but I didn't care. This was what I loved, being a minister, growing a church. I didn't know at the time that this would be the training I needed to run Center for Spiritual Living Kaua'i.

As I grew in this job, Rev. Chris continued to treat me pretty harshly. I just wasn't perfect enough for him and he pointed it out all the time. It was probably the hardest job I ever had and many of the things he said might have been true. All my inadequacies and insecurities erupted like a volcano. We fought. I screamed back at him. On one particular day, everything came to a head. I don't even remember what it was about but I just walked into my office and slammed the door, crying. I remember singing *Just You Wait!* from *My Fair Lady*. I was always the actress...so dramatic!

Later that day, Rev. Chris found me in the lobby and we had it out. It finally was clear that the reason I was always so upset about being perfect for this job was because I cared so much. Maybe it was karmic. Maybe it was a past life. It didn't make sense. If anyone else had been spoken to the way I was, they would have quit. If anyone was as unhappy with someone as he was with me, they would have fired that person. We just kept going. We worked out our karma. I never blamed him. I lost my victimhood. I took all of it and grew through it. I got really strong. As I said, we remain the best of friends to this day. If you asked him about this, he'd probably say I was his best administrator, outside of my dear friend Rev. Dr. Dean. Hindsight is an amazing revealer and time does heal all wounds.

This was a huge transformational experience for me. I saw it through for the same reason that I do everything. I love this philosophy and I practice it. I'm going to take responsibility for all my experiences. I'm going to find my way through any mess and come out at the other end a better and bigger person in consciousness. I hadn't learned all I needed to learn from the Rev. Chris-Rita Andriello experience. When I did, I'd be ready for something more. We can't run from our challenges. As we know, wherever we go, there we are. I wasn't going to do that ever again.

There was much more happening in this time in my life. It would make a great book. I'd call it *From Victim to Victor*. Being a victim isn't always about what you think it is. Rev. Chris used to say, "If you are a victim, you'll find your perpetrator." It's true, and to this day, I find myself in the perpetrator position on many occasions. I don't put myself there. Someone gives me that authority. I really get this now. If you show up as a victim, a perpetrator is born.

Even with the job title of "Administrator/Assistant Minister," I didn't really get to do all that much ministering. It was mostly administrative. I'm grateful for that now because it is where I learned to run a church. I didn't get to preach or teach much but there is more to running a church. The preaching and teaching parts come easily to me. It's the other part that takes training—the financial ups and downs, the people's demands, remaining in a kind, calm state when you really want to mouth off to someone, learning patience and humility, learning to stand in your power, working all hours of the day and night, staying in Principle no matter what, growing bigger than anything in front of you. It is those things and so much more that I began to learn in my training as Rev. Chris's Assistant Minister and Administrator. It wouldn't be until I became a senior minister myself that I would truly go through my ministerial rite of passage. That would be coming soon.

Patrick and I knew from the very day we received our ministerial licenses we would eventually start our own work. It was 2012 and we were getting to the point that we couldn't grow in Los Angeles under someone else's ministry. As a minister, unless you are willing to jump out onto a limb and take over another pulpit or start your own church or even be a focus minister, you are part of someone else's ministry and vision. You must remain loyal and supportive. You are never going to have the freedom and creative vision that comes from starting your own work. This is fine for some, but Patrick and I are creatives. We'd already proven that in our lives over and over. It was time for another leap of faith. We could not live up to our full and true potential in Los Angeles.

But where would we go? How would we do it? The place and time were about to reveal themselves. After fifteen years of growing up in Los Angeles, our journey would now take a new and even more difficult turn. When we are ready for the new journey, it appears. We always have the opportunity to decline it, but it does appear. If we decide to say yes, it doesn't mean it's going to be easy, but for us it was going to be the most exciting and fulfilling journey of a lifetime.

I was still trying to keep my red dress on which seemed to float in and out of my closet. I realize that sometimes we let go of who we truly are. We get scared. We are afraid to make a decision that will cause drastic change in our life. Who knew I would put my red dress back on under the guise of ministry and on the island of Kaua'i?

Chapter 16

Ministers, Eunuchs, and Other Societal Roles

It takes a great deal of courage and independence to decide to design your own image instead of the one that society rewards, but it gets easier as you go along.

~Germaine Greer, The Female Eunuch

We left for Kaua`i in 2013 and here we are eleven years later after having thrived spiritually, emotionally, and mentally through many physical and financial challenges. Our philosophy of the Science of Mind keeps us solidly planted in Principle. This book's content is not about ministry in general or our ministry of founding and running a spiritual center. These memoirs are in another book in the making called *You Had No Idea and Neither Did We.* I will only write about ministry regarding how it applies to my red dress.

I titled this chapter *Ministers, Eunuchs, and other Societal Roles* to summarize the feelings I sometimes pick up surrounding ministry and sexuality. I know that a eunuch is a male who has been castrated but I wonder if women can become eunuchs, metaphorically speaking, when they are ostracized for appearing sexy or flirtatious? It is not a physical castration, but instead, a mental and emotional one. I think there is something to examine here.

While writing this book I received a call from one of my mainland friends concerning a talk I had given. "I love the way you were dressed today," she said. "You looked just like a minister." She meant it as a compliment and I was not surprised by this remark. There is a dress code for ministry. It's a silent one. It's not written anywhere but if you look at the pictures of different female ministers, you will see they all dress similarly—suits, high necked dresses, pants suits, shoulders draped with shawls, etc. The silent dress code is not only for ministers. I believe it stems from a broader view on what is appropriate dress for women and the consequences she might suffer based on what she is wearing.

In an article in *Psychology Today* entitled *Was She Asking for It*, Wendy L. Patrick (J.D., Ph.D., career trial attorney, behavioral analyst, author of Red Flags, and co-author of Reading People) wrote:

> Decades ago, Ed M. Edmonds and Delwin D. Cahoon (1986) investigated public attitudes related to victim attire. Participants were shown slides featuring a female model wearing clothes that were either sexy or unsexy, then asked questions about whether the model might be robbed or raped. Participants believed that the model wearing sexy clothes was

more likely to be robbed or raped, provoke an attack, and be responsible for her victimization. Participants also viewed the assailant as less accountable if the woman was assaulted while wearing sexy clothes rather than sexually conservative clothing.

Delahunty-Goodman and Graham also cited research by Cassidy and Hurrell (1995) examining the impact of victim clothing on judgments of date rape, "finding that participants who viewed a photograph of the victim in 'provocative' clothing were more likely to believe she was responsible for the behavior of her assailant, more likely to view the assailant's behavior as justified, and less likely to recognize rape. They cite a recent study of date rape that found participants attributed more responsibility for rape to a victim pictured in a short skirt than a moderate or long-length skirt." (Workman & Freeburg, 1999)

And in another article in *Medium: It's Time to Stop Judging Women By Their Clothes,* Gaya Tri Aryä wrote this:

Women should not have to worry about being judged or harassed when wearing whatever they want. It's time to change the way we think about women who dress provocatively and accept that what they wear doesn't necessarily indicate their value or consent. Let's work to create a society that is more tolerant and diverse.

I recently heard Barbra Streisand talk on this subject in the audio version of her new book, *My Name Is Barbra*. She was criticized for wearing something too sexy at a formal public occasion. She shared that she thought men should take responsibility for their own sexual feelings when seeing a sexily dressed woman. "Can't they control their own urges?" was her sentiment. I remember a man who was in sales telling me he thought his women competitors got more business because of their physical appearance and dress. There is much to debate here and we all, both men and women, have our opinions.

Where do you stand on how you dress? Do you dress to fit in? What are your feelings about your way of dressing and how you feel about your body? Do you care what others think? Do you dress in what makes you feel empowered, sexy, and beautiful? Do you think about how lowcut your blouse or dress might be? How do you feel about how other women dress? Do you judge them? I'd love for you to explore these questions for yourself. I think it matters and gives an indication of how you feel about your sensual self. Why do some of us hide our bodies under layers of clothes? No matter our body type, I believe we can learn to feel comfortable in our bodies. How we dress makes a difference and why we dress a certain way indicates a lot about our mental attitude.

For me, it's been a journey. I've gone from feeling very natural in my choices of dress to feeling judged. I've gone from going braless without a thought, to grabbing my bra and putting it on, not because I wanted to, but because I thought I should. I think our comfort level surrounding the way we dress started a long time ago as children. What our parents felt about their bodies was passed on to us. I never saw my mother or father naked. I was constantly warned about my choice of clothing. I wanted a bikini which was just starting to become popular in the sixties. I remember the song: *Itsy Bitsy Teenie Weenie Yellow Polka Dot Bikini* sung by Brian Hyland.

If you haven't heard it, check out the YouTube video: http://tiny.cc/bqxwzz You'll be quite shocked at what was acceptable in those days regarding how we treat our children. We were definitely trying to come out of our puritanical age, but not necessarily in a healthy way.

One of my best friends was European. She was so free with her body in a healthy, innocent way. She helped to balance my feelings about dress, nudity, and freedom regarding body image. I recall the encounter I had with a friend who was taking my professional headshot when I was a Mormon. She was shocked by the way I had become so modest.

When I was growing up, I remember a little girl of five who innocently ran through the sprinklers, played in her pool, and even went to the beach topless. Her little bikini brief created a stir in the neighborhood. "Put something on her," was the cry. Because her parents didn't want their child to endure insults, they put her bikini top on. I wonder how that affected that little girl. Since a child is a subconscious sponge before the age of eight, I can only imagine that somewhere in the recesses of her subconscious, she might have accepted the fact that something was wrong with feeling free in her body. It might have also created a contradiction between what her parents taught her and what was socially acceptable. If it wasn't addressed immediately, I think she would have carried that moment into adulthood.

My own daughter played in her backyard pool in the nude. She was innocent and free. What takes away this feeling of naturalness in our skin? I believe it is growing up and integrating into society and its judgments. We are social creatures, and if we feel unaccepted by the tribe, it can make us refugees left in the wilderness. We have a strong longing to be accepted.

At times I felt I needed to forgive myself for bringing my daughters up to be free in their bodies. Yet their lives have shown me they have no problem knowing when to dress "appropriately" while at the same time being free enough to let go of a bra when it is right for them. When I speak to my oldest, she is grateful for the freedom she feels about her body and bodies in general. She said, "It's just the way it was in our house." I also remember meeting with a therapist and discussing nudity in our home. She scrutinized and questioned us if there was child abuse at home. This was not the truth and we were finally able to convince her. And when our children became old enough and felt the pull of modesty, that was okay too. We grew and evolved together with open conversation.

I never thought much about what was appropriate—whether my shoulders were exposed or whether my dress was low cut or too short until it began to be pointed out to me. It was not about appropriate dress for an occasion but more about the exposure of my body. I remember wearing a white leather miniskirt and strapless top under my gown at my college graduation. I never thought about or cared whether I was being judged...until I did care. Stars like Madonna, Lady Gaga, and others have brought women's sexuality into the forefront in very explicit ways. I am grateful for them and I have also judged them at times.

What has compounded these issues for me was becoming a minister. I remember when I first came to Kaua'i and wore some of my more sensual clothing to conduct our Sunday services, no one ever said a word. Yet I did feel a bit self-conscious. Were ministers supposed to dress a certain way? I was not trained that way by my openly gay mentor who reveled in all his practitioners and ministers dressing fun and sexily.

Early on in my ministry on Kaua'i, I remember putting a shawl around my shoulders to cover a spaghetti strap dress. One of my close friends, a male who was verbally forthcoming, came up to me and asked me point-blank, "Why are you covering yourself up? You look beautiful and elegant. I can't tell you what to do but I think you should shed the shawl." I appreciated his advice and compliment. I did remove the shawl, but since I became a minister, I still have body shame at times.

Here is one example that made me really think. Because of the time difference between Kaua'i and the mainland, I often find myself in Zoom meetings at early hours, sometimes as early as 4 a.m. Because Kaua'i is a very hot and tropical climate, I often dress in a sarong around the house. During a particular class with my ministerial friends, because of the level of the screen and the way the sarong was tied, I appeared to be naked. Of course I wasn't and my class often joked about this and called me "Naked Rita." I actually liked the nickname and so did they. These were, for the most part, colleagues and friends in ministry that I knew well.

One day I was on a Zoom call at 5 a.m. with a group of ministers, spiritual practitioners, and other spiritual leaders in the New Thought movement. I didn't know these people well so I made sure my sarong was modestly tied around my neck, exposing only my bare shoulders. As the Zoom call began, there was a slight chill in the 70-degree air so I pulled a shawl around my shoulders. The class progressed and the room was getting warmer. I wanted to take my shawl off but I unexpectantly felt exposed. Was this too exposed for the group I was with? In that moment I stopped myself. I almost had to force myself to pull that shawl down from around my shoulders. Was this self-consciousness surrounding my dress choices still prevalent in my subconscious, perhaps lingering from my Mormon days or those moments with my father when he criticized me in my red dress? Obviously it was, but I was conscious now. I looked at everyone else on the screen and they were all modestly dressed in tee shirts and button up blouses and shirts. I felt out of place even though no one was saying anything. This interaction between me and my shawl needed to be investigated. Why was I so uncomfortable in my own skin? My high-collared, capped-sleeved Mormon days came back in a flash and the question still prevailed. Why must women be made to feel too seductive or provocative because their bodice was low cut or their shoulders exposed?

I found an article online that addressed this issue. Female lawyers were discussing *Bare Arms at Work: Yea Or Nay?* The internet magazine was called *Corporette for Overachiev-*

ing Chicks. Kat Griffin is the founder, publisher, and editor-in-chief. The name of the magazine was enough to rouse my curiosity. I dug a little deeper. The dialogue going back and forth and the survey brought forth the question of what was the appropriate sleeveless attire for the workplace? The verdict was: the less arm or shoulder showing, the better. I'm not comparing my early morning Zoom calls with lawyers in the courtroom, nor am I suggesting tank tops in the workplace, but still what is it with a woman's shoulders that cries out for them to be hidden? Are they just too kissable?

In an article in the *NY Times* entitled *What is Appropriate Work Dress? Readers Respond,* this comment from Lesley Potts capsulized the feelings of those who responded.

> The school district I work for implemented a dress code after a teacher turned up for a meeting in shorts, flip-flops and a tank top, upsetting the superintendent. They went totally the other way and now sleeveless anything isn't allowed for women and they even got into sandals and what percentage of foot could be visible. No denim, period. It's relaxed a little since that superintendent left, but the sleeveless thing...this is Georgia y'all and it's as hot as Hades half the year.

It seems to be "much ado about nothing." I was a teacher for a time and we also had a dress code. The consensus in many of the articles I perused was that different parts of the country and world hold different standards. Dress accordingly. My original question remains. What makes how a person dresses appropriate or inappropriate? Who created the criteria? And who is responsible for that criteria? If it is just about being neat and clean and respectful to the occasion, I understand, but if it is about the lure of one's clothing, then I am back where I started. Why are we hiding the curves of our bodies?

I always appreciated my mentor and friend, Rev. Chris from Los Angeles, a gay man who was a minister, married, and father of two children. He would encourage all of us to wear sexy clothing. Low cut dresses and heels were all the rage. He promoted our uniqueness and sensuality in a healthy way. There was no fuss about it. We just were who we were. There was a bohemian quality to our group and I fit in perfectly. Why shouldn't we just be comfortable in our skin? I recently heard a minister of New Thought give a talk called *Let's Talk About Sex, Baby!* She was in her eighties, and in it she called us all "yummy" as our sexual, sensual selves. I really appreciated her openness.

One time a superior minister was visiting my center in Los Angeles to check on Rev. Chris and the advancement of his Center. As his assistant, I was to meet her and take her around. I remember very purposefully wearing what I thought was the most modest dress I had. That dress's length went to my calves, but it did have a low curve at my breasts. She commented about how a minister/practitioner should dress. She didn't acknowledge my clothing but I knew she was talking about me. I later found out she used to be a nun. Can you see how our background affects everything?

Everything is an opinion, based on how we grew up and were acclimatized by family and society.

This next article took the way a woman dresses to be a reflection of her intelligence. Wow!

Anyway, this seemingly parodic piece links to an admittedly far more legitimate study published in Yale Scientific, which did find an inverse correlation between the amount of skin shown and perceptions of the person's intelligence and competence. Many of the experiments conducted jointly by University of Maryland, Yale University and Northeastern University "confirm the notion that we may perceive more scantily clad people as less competent." Now, in India, where I grew up, women belonging to certain religions and communities tend to dress more conservatively than others. So, although I was never raised with the idea that a woman's arms needed to be kept covered for reasons of modesty, I do know it's a pretty common thing. But it seems now that bare arms are an apparent reflection of not just our modesty but also our competency. What's up with that?

~from Do Women Need to Cover Their Shoulders to be Respected? Fashion magazine staffers discuss former Prime Minister Kim

Campbell's divisive tweet ~Pahull Bains and
Greg Hudson

Where am I going with this? I'm just trying to free us from
dogma and judgment. I'm trying to take us out of our cages
of false modesty and let us know that we have discernment.
We have good judgment. We know how to dress, when to
dress a certain way, and why. We know ourselves. I believe
there is nothing wrong with wanting to feel sexy. There is
no reason why desiring to look and feel sexy and sensual
should be an excuse for someone else to feel uncomfortable,
or worse yet, to hurt you.

Perhaps we all might take responsibility for our feelings
and respect for our bodies and everyone else's. Can you
imagine how the world would feel if everyone took responsibility for their own emotions, feelings, and thoughts? That's
what the whole New Thought philosophy centers on. This
is what the new science—quantum science—is teaching us.
What we tell ourselves affects our brains and causes us to
look for everything to confirm those beliefs and thoughts.
The way we think and the way we perceive our world is
affecting everything. It is either expanding us as a species or
keeping us stuck in the old ineffective way of thinking that
causes bullying, war, and the like. We point at our leaders,
calling them corrupt, but we are the ones who placed them
there with our lost sense of self. It is a macrocosm of the
microcosm.

I believe it is time to embrace ourselves as spiritual, sexy,
and emotionally stable women and men. The only way to do

this is to dive deep into our psyche and bring up everything to be healed that needs healing. As we do that, we will discover our True Self and all the restrictions and condemnations that cover up that True Self will fall away. Like the Golden Buddha covered by moss and dirt, we too will reveal our gold.

Can we cast off our childhood traumas and turn them into prayers of thanksgiving? Can we leave those traumas behind and see them for what they were: confused people with no one to guide their path, trying to understand what they were feeling. I'm on a mission to understand. At the same time, I do not want to throw out the baby with the bathwater, but instead to bring her up and really look at her. What if that baby can be washed clean of all taboos and stand truly naked and beautiful and free? I do think it is possible. I think it might be the healthiest thing we do for society. However, it might have to happen one person at a time and they must be willing to take that deep dive into their own psyche.

Can we be spiritual and sexual at the same time? Is sensuality our spiritual nature? Mother Nature is very sensual. I accept her as such. The warm breezes that caress us on a hot summer night and the wave of the palm trees here on Kaua'i are most definitely sensual and elegant at the same time. The ocean water, when truly embodied, deeply fills us with its holy, salty essence. Just a few weekends ago, I had the opportunity to enter a Himalayan salt cave and enjoy a guided meditation. It was spiritual and sensual at the same time. Are we willing to feel all our feelings and to stop segregating them into either "good" or "bad"?

How can we express ourselves, sensually speaking, and not feel judged or less than? Can we eat a piece of cheesecake or a pastry and allow the crème to be enjoyed as sensually as a kiss? My husband had a female friend who used to relish her food. One day in a restaurant, she ate so slowly, acknowledging the deliciousness and sensuality of eating, that the waiter noticed it and commented on her ability to truly enjoy the food. Is it too sexy to eat food and feel at one with the experience in a deep and sensual way? These are all questions I ask myself. These things seem natural to me, yet I stop myself, afraid of being observed as I was by my father that day in the dress shop or as the Mormon women saw me and whispered about me in the corridors of our church. When will I give up and not care? When will I claim my body as God's body and allow myself to relish my sensuality and aliveness? I turned seventy-one this year and I do not want to waste another moment. I want to wake up to the gift of sensuality and share it with everyone who will listen.

Chapter 17

Keeping Secrets at My Own Expense

Listen...do you want to know a secret?...Do you promise not to tell?

~ John Lennon and Paul McCartney, sung by George Harrison

As we get older, even when there are times we need to keep others in the dark, secrets can stir up feelings of regret, shame, and guilt. We might be hiding shopping bills from our partner or keeping our new promotion hush-hush because our friend just lost her job. Whatever the reason, past research has shown the psychological effects of keeping secrets include a range of negative outcomes from depression and anxiety to lower relationship satisfaction and poor physical health.

~Nandina Maharaj, Psychology Today

As I write this book, I am telling secrets I have kept for much of my life. Some of these secrets like the one that concerned my older man have been kept for over fifty years. When I first entered that relationship at age fourteen, the first thing he told me was, "Don't tell anyone." The reason I was given was, "They won't understand." Of course, now I know that if I had told that secret, it would have brought serious consequences to him. I felt his trust and I reveled in the secret. I never thought of telling it to my parents or any elders in my life. However, secrets are not met to be kept and I longed to let it out. As a love-crazed teenager, I told one of my close friends. She thought it was exciting and romantic. We even had a nickname for him so that we could talk about him when others were around. I disclosed the secret to a nun at my school during a sex education class. I don't remember why I told her or her trying to stop me or doing anything about it at all. I only recall that she told me I shouldn't be having sex before marriage and she warned me about possible pregnancy. Maybe things were looked at differently in the 1960s. Think of the MeToo Movement now and how many years it took for those women and men to come forward with their secrets. We certainly held those secrets at our own expense.

I have felt some trepidation in telling my story in this book, even though I have done my best to either protect the characters by changing the names or circumstance or by offering a positive understanding of the situations. Even now, I am holding back on publishing. What will people think of me? Will they think of me differently now that they know my past?

I've titled this chapter *Keeping Secrets at My Own Expense* because I think that when we keep secrets, we hold a part of ourselves hostage. That part of us remains in prison behind the bars of shame, self-loathing, and self-judgment. My feeling is that I must release myself from my self-made prison through the telling of this story. My hope is that those reading this who might be going through a similar experience or feeling guilt or shame over their past might seek assistance in processing their own story. I hope that they might finally be freed from their self-made prison. I really think it is important for us to tell our stories to each other, not to complain, but to help process ourselves and each other into healing. I have done my best to tell my story with that in mind.

In an article called *Why Abuse Survivors Stay Silent* on the *Psych Central* website written by Brittany Van Der Bill, many reasons are given as to why those who are abused remain silent. I never remained totally silent but coming out now has brought out some of these feelings with it.

> **Shame** can play a significant role in keeping survivors silent. Survivors may believe that the abuse was somehow their fault or that they caused it. They might also feel embarrassed or ashamed that they didn't or couldn't defend themselves.

In the case of what I experienced as a teenager, I do feel there was shame surrounding it. Perhaps I didn't feel that at the time but now I question whether it was truly abuse or whether I brought it upon myself because of my behavior. It took me thirty years to even think of the possibility that it could be abuse. When I deeply reflect upon it, I know it wasn't right for an adult to take advantage of a child but I can also make many excuses for it being okay.

> **Judgment** Sometimes a survivor may be afraid that other people are going to negatively judge them.

With regard to feeling judged, I do believe that this is a big reason why I didn't tell anyone at the time. I was told, "They won't understand." In my young mind, who would understand what I was going through. They might try to stop me and I surely didn't want that to happen. Many years later when my father asked me, "Did he ever touch you?" I denied telling the truth for fear that my father would judge me.

> **They feel responsible.** Sometimes a person might not report abuse because they feel responsible for it.

This was most definitely the case. I did feel like I was responsible for the whole thing. There was a part of me—my conscience—that knew I might be hurting his family. Why would I tell them and hurt them now? Would they blame me? Was I responsible for keeping this secret for him?

Downplaying abuse. They might downplay the abuse or not even consider that they were abused.

This was probably the biggest reason I never told my story. I never considered it abuse until my teacher and mentor pointed out to me that it was. I was in my forties and even then I denied it. It was the first story I told David when we met. He never told me I was abused. David and I remained friends with this man throughout our marriage. Wow! I'm thinking about all this now and realizing how far I've come on the path of self-healing and self-love.

So, what about the other secrets in this book? What about my three-way relationships and especially the way my relationship with Patrick began? These were not abusive but still they were secrets I kept—we kept. David was open to telling everyone in the beginning about our relationship with Patrick, but as soon as the breakup occurred it became a secret. David even denied it happened. This is one of the reasons that we do not remain friends. What if his new family finds out? There was a code of silence surrounding what was at one time revealed in freedom. I'm sad about that.

At present, in Patrick's and my case, why didn't we tell? For us it was about people misinterpreting who we are now. We didn't want people to think we were swingers. We aren't. I remember we told one couple about it over dinner. They were in the film business and we were discussing the screenplay I had written, *Breaking All the Rules*. The couple wouldn't leave our house that night. They just kept lingering. Finally, at 2 a.m., we had to ask them to leave. Were they waiting for something to happen between the four of us? We surmised that they were. They tried to get together with us after that but we declined. After that night we never told anyone. Well, I say never told anyone, but we did disclose it in our ministerial class when we were openly discussing our pasts in a confidential setting. Our ministerial cohorts still joke with us, hinting that maybe we are keeping up with this lifestyle.

Through the writing of this book, I will finally share the beginnings of my relationship with Patrick. It feels good to be able to talk about it freely. As I grow older, what I am feeling is that my secrets were born out of wanting to be accepted on all levels. What I know is if I tell my truth and I am rejected or judged, then more than likely that person or persons do not belong in my life. I want to be free to be known completely. My children already know, and no matter their feelings about it, I am glad I do not have to keep secrets from them. My parents kept plenty of secrets from me and I never had the opportunity to really know them. I think that is a loss for all of us.

I am trusting that in the writing of this book I have been respectful to everyone involved and that for every past secret that I have revealed, there has been a truth that has been received that is helpful to the reader's life. That has been my intention, and in the process, I have healed much shame, guilt, and judgment of myself.

Chapter 18

The Red Dress IS My Holy Grail

You must choose. But choose wisely, for as the true Grail will bring you life; the false Grail will take it from you.

~Indiana Jones and the Last Crusade film

While writing this book I have made a discovery. It is not something I had previously planned to write nor did I think of it in this way before. However, it makes total sense given the fact that my entire life has been about revealing the Real me—the sensual me and the sexual me all wrapped up in the spiritual me. This might seem surprising, but when I first began writing, I still hadn't found my red dress nor did I know what it was. During this process, by revealing the "Self to the self," as Ernest Holmes would put it, I made a great discovery.

(When I say the "Self to the self," I am talking about our Divine Self or Higher Self helping us to let go of the ego mind or the small self; the mind that judges us and everyone else).

Finding my red dress is a metaphorical representation of the Real me. It is not just the sexual me or the need to release my sensual nature. The red dress is all of me. It is my Holy Grail. Many of us know the story of King Arthur and the Knights of the Round Table. The grail originates in the story as the Holy Cup that Jesus drank from at the Last Supper. The knight who found the grail would also find the healing elixir that it contained.

> From the knights of medieval legends to Indiana Jones, the holy grail has been the most sought-after Christian relic in popular culture for centuries. The grail is most commonly identified as the cup that Jesus drank from at the Last Supper and that Joseph of Arimathea used to collect Jesus's blood when he was crucified. Given the importance of Jesus's crucifixion and the eucharist in Christian beliefs, the search for the grail became the holiest of quests, as it signified the pursuit of union with God. ~from *History.com*

> The Grail is described as having a wide range of spiritual and magical attributes, but is also thought of as an ultimate object of achievement or desire. ~from *Learnreligions.com*

We might say that we seek to have abundance or good health or love in our life, but truly, what I believe we seek is wholeness. The grail as the holy object is a perfect metaphor for those of us who seek to find what makes us feel whole.

In my faith, the Science of Mind, the "Real Me" is God. It is the Christ within me, my oneness with all, and that which makes me whole. The Christ within me is not the man Jesus; it is the unalterable knowing that I am one *of* God. It encompasses my shadows and my light. As the light shines on my shadow side, I am all light. My shadows are the wounds that I have healed from a lifetime of inner work. This Holy Grail is the most precious of gifts for each and every one of us.

What is your grail? Is it possible that the search could be over right now? I believe it already is as soon as we decide that it is. Your Holy Grail is your Real you. It is all of you as you present yourself authentically and transparently to the world.

I'm often asked by clients, "How do I stop struggling? How do I release my past? How do I stop this inner scolding voice that continues to tell me I am not worth it?" All of this is a wall that separates us from our wholeness. For a lifetime, I have asked myself these same questions. The answers are found in knowing my identity as God. God is not a superior being but a Presence that reveals Itself through all of us. To know this, I must accept every part of myself without labeling it good or bad. It is about surrendering and turning myself over to my greatness.

Ralph Waldo Emerson, the great philosopher, writer, and Transcendentalist wrote this, "Let us take our bloated nothingness out of the path of the divine circuits." In my early study of metaphysics, many of my classmates hated this quote. They found it derogatory and demeaning. This has always been one of my favorite Emerson quotes. I don't think my fellow classmates truly understood what Emerson was saying.

Many times in my life when I have needed to raise my vibration a notch or when I have felt bogged down by self-condemnation, I have felt the vibration of my "bloated nothingness." What is our "bloated nothingness"? It is that nothingness that we have dreamed up as real. It is merely a thought or what we think of ourselves. When we decide to release it as a thought, it no longer can concretize as our lives. I have learned in Spiritual Practitioner training to reduce everything that is troubling the client, whether it is health, poverty, or the like, to a thought. Once we reduce things to a thought, we can truly change the thought. "Thoughts are things," and we are not our thoughts; we are the thinker. It is just a thought. It is "bloated nothingness." Ernest Holmes wrote, "Do not give into that belief—not even for a second —because it is nothing but a thought which says you cannot heal. Nothing but a thought is saying, or could be saying it, and since it is only a thought which says it, it is only a thought which can unsay it." ~*Science of Mind,* page 199

As I have come to learn in the study of quantum theory, everything is energy and everything is fluid and ever-changing. Downward causation means that everything in the world of effects is here due to the consciousness of the individual and the Collective. Everything is the dream we dream it up to be. Whatever we observe shows up for us just as we perceive it. We can continue to play out our old dramas and we will repeat them. I've proven that over and over as you might have gathered while reading this book. We are powerful dreamers. Paul Levy, in his book *The Quantum Revelation*, quotes Banesh Hoffman from *The Strange Story of the Quantum*, published in 1947:

> Now is the terrible crisis of our civilization. Now is the fateful hour of high decision. For better or worse, We, the People of Earth, must choose our future. Quantum physics tells us that the future is not written in stone, but instead is indeterminate and filled with infinite potential. How the world of the quantum manifests depends on how we dream it. As it says in the Bible Deuteronomy 30:19, "I have set before you life and death, blessing and curse, therefore, choose life, that both you and thy seed may live." The choice is truly ours.

Is our life a blessing or a curse? The choice is ours. As a real example, let me take the experience I had with my older man during my teenage years. What if I continue to hold onto how wronged I was and how I wish I could have changed that experience or wish it had never happened? What good would that do me? What if I let it shield me from my sensuality because I feel dirty or unclean because of that experience? This would be an example of my "bloated nothingness" getting in the way of the Divine circuits. Instead, can I still acknowledge the experience, feel sadness surrounding it, and then merely switch my perspective on it?

What if he was doing the best he knew how? What if I was doing the best I knew how? What if, instead, I focused on that pure young girl who ran up the mountains of New York and ran in the streams of Long Island, feeling her oneness with nature? What if that is what attracted this person to her? What if he was just wanting that freeing nature for himself and he took it without thinking of the consequences of his actions, not intending to hurt her at all? Please do not confuse this with saying everyone can do whatever they want to another person. That would be arguing for your limitations. I believe it is not mentally or spiritually healthy to hold on to bitterness and shame.

I choose a different road for myself. Sometimes I have felt sad about that experience. I even wish it hadn't happened. However, what I know is that it is part of my history and I do not want to remove any part of my past. What I do want to remove is any shadow or condemnation concerning the incident. I want to forgive everyone involved, especially myself. One might ask, how do I forgive...*even that?* You may know what I'm talking about—that experience you might have had that was so horrific that you can't even think about it. It remains hidden in the dark. In order to heal it, we have to feel it. We have to sit with it and allow ourselves to be healed. We have to want to be healed. Of course, sometimes deep psychological work is needed and there are professionals available to all of us. If we want our wholeness, we must begin the work.

I have learned a very powerful forgiveness exercise by Rev. Dr. Harry Morgan Moses, a Science of Mind minister. I'm not sure if he created it or adopted it from some other spiritual practice. If you choose to use this exercise, please do this with someone you trust completely. I wouldn't suggest doing it by yourself. You need support.

1. Bring up the person/incident you want to let go of. In as much detail as possible, describe it and state how it made you feel.

2. Where do you feel it in your body?

3. In first person, pretending you are talking to the person you conceive as having hurt you, state how you would have liked it to be instead. An example would be: "I would have preferred you would have respected me..." Come up with as many scenarios of your preference as you can, in as much detail as possible.

4. Now, as you push your arms forward and away from you and downward in dismissal, say, "I cancel my expectations of you ever having... (put in the words of that which you would have preferred.) For example, "I cancel my expectations of you ever having respected me..." Say it as many times as you need until you feel it.

5. Then state, "I now return to you your part in this experience, and I release you to your highest and best journey."

6. Then bless the person and yourself using your form of prayer.

This is a powerful exercise. Sometimes it has to be repeated many times before you truly feel the release. I invite you to be willing to repeat it as many times as you need to. It will definitely aid you in releasing your "bloated nothingness" and move your life forward in a new and powerful direction.

As I continue to deepen my understanding and acceptance of myself and forgiveness of my past, I believe I am truly receiving that Holy Grail that I have sought my whole life. When I do, I proudly wear my red dress, literally and figuratively, for all to see. I accept my God-Self and proudly reveal her and her creative self to the world. I feel that I have revealed her and embraced her in this book. I have been honest and forthcoming and authentic. I trust it has helped you on your journey.

Epilogue

Women and Men are birthless, deathless and ageless Spirit. ...This leaves nothing to be born, mature, decay and die. Life cannot grow old. God—in us, and through us, as us—can only express according to Its Own Nature, which is Perfection.

~Ernest Holmes

As I finish this book, I am seventy-one years old. I have gone through menopause and all those transitions and changes in our bodies that we experience on life's journey. Through it all, I've always had a deep appreciation and love for my body. I've had one belief that I know has allowed me to thrive. I know that aging can be a graceful and a health-filled process. I do not have to give into any collective consciousness concerning its effects on my body. I can grow old with as much vitality as is required for me to live a healthy and joy-filled life. Perhaps this belief was born when I witnessed my seventy-year-old father, bare-chested in his swimming trunks, flexing his muscles in front of a mirror and turning to me with a big smile to let me know in his thick Italian accent, "Us Andriellos, we get younger with age!" It was one of his authoritative suggestions that I took in whole-heartedly. Thank you, Daddy!

My voice teacher once told me I'd "grow into my face." I don't know if that was a compliment but I took it as one. I feel beautiful. I take care of my body with exercise and good nutrition but I know health goes far beyond the physical world. It is our attitude about ourselves that lead the way to our physiology. It is our ability to heal our past traumas and live in our joy that make the real difference in how we age. The more we can smile from truth, the less we wrinkle.

I know a lady who is one hundred years old. She is one of the most beautiful older ladies I have ever known. Aging is not just about staying sexually active but it is about staying sensually attuned. This woman's secret to her long vibrant life, she says, is gratitude. She says this with tears in her eyes. She has lost many loved ones during her life span but she chooses to give thanks for everything. Albert Schweitzer wrote, "Think with deep gratitude of those who have lighted the flames within us." This woman lives this quote and you witness it in the glow of her skin and the sparkle of her eyes.

As I continue to take the journey of aging, I feel good in my body and I still enjoy a healthy, deeply intimate sex life. I'm grateful. I am not alone. I give gratitude every day for the companionship of Patrick who totally accepts me for all that I am. This could never happen if I did not accept myself first.

I happen to hang with women who feel good about aging. I do my best to encourage those who come to me for help. There is much research out there on older women living fully, sexually and sensually, way beyond their menopausal years.

> There's a myth that women stop having sex after menopause, and it's completely untrue. Women are still able to receive and give pleasure as much, if not more, than they previously were. ~Lexx Brown-James, Ph.D., licensed marriage and family therapist

I remember my own seventy-year-old mother, after my father passed away, revealing her excitement about her upcoming second marriage by showing me her sexy nightie that she would wear on her wedding night. She was so joy-filled and continued to be all through her seventies and into her eighties with her new partner.

There is also plenty of negative information and warnings out there about what to expect as we age. There are plenty of suggestions to prolong our youth and increase our libido as well as plastic surgery to preserve our image. I'm not against anything that makes us feel good about our bodies and ourselves. We each should follow our own intuition about what we do with our bodies.

As for me, I do not subscribe to the negative information or the warnings of things to come. As I know from practicing the Science of Mind and Quantum Physics, everything is perception. Everything that occurs in our life is occurring because of our beliefs and feelings. For example, I went through menopause with none of the serious symptoms I was warned about. For medical reasons, I was not able to take any hormone therapy so I created my own. My hormone therapy was joy, practicing my creativity, having fun, following my bliss, and enjoying a healthy sex life.

As you age, what do you believe about sex? Or as a younger person, do you have notions about how it will be? Do you feel sensual even without an active sex life? Are you comfortable in your skin no matter your shape and size? I want this for all women. I have met and witnessed women far younger than myself having given up on life and romance, but I also know I am not alone in my positivity. I am fortunate to know very many healthy, sexually-active women and men in their sixties, seventies, and even eighties. I understand that we are born into race suggestion about aging but I also know that it is up to us. Genes do not turn themselves on and off. Dr. Bruce Lipton's *Biology of Belief* explains this concept of "epigenetics."

What have we decided for ourselves? What's important to us? Have we claimed our red dresses, our wholeness, our Holy Grail? My intention for my life going forward is to be healthy and joyful. My intention is to take all that I know about the power of the mind and actually use it to have the best experience of living while I am in this body. I know this is possible for everyone. We might not be able to have our twenty-year-old bodies at seventy, but we can have the best and most healthy body at any age. We might not be engaged in an intimate sexual relationship but we can feel our own sensuality. We can experience self-love in every moment. We can choose to empower ourselves by wearing our red dresses proudly and with the intention to revel in all of life.

Acknowledgments

Everyone on our life's path is our teacher. I believe we come here with a soul group, and they show up in many forms—in different people and, yes, even pets. In my seventy-one years, my soul group has been vast, individualized, and has definitely assisted me in finding my "Red Dress."

Firstly, thank you to my beautiful husband, lover, friend, and fellow journeyer, Patrick Feren. Thank you for coming into my life, for taking this wild ride with me, and for holding true to our vow to always embrace change. I love you madly!

On another note, writing a book with this level of vulnerability was deeply challenging and, yes, frightening to release for others to read. How would they react? It took an immense amount of trust, and the people listed below showed up for me with honesty and love. Thank you to Dana Craig Baier, Dr. Liza Marquez, Terry Sheehan, Isha Doellgast, Beverly Eager, Deb Valentina, Dr. Lori Savage, and Sue Buckley.

I thank my parents who brought me to this earth and played a crucial role in the beginning of my spiritual journey. Although I eventually turned away from the religion in which I was raised, it provided a foundation for my path toward wholeness and a deeper connection with God.

Thank you to my siblings, Maria, Gregory, and Paul, who walked the path of growing up with me.

Thank you to the special angels in my life, my Aunt Lucile and my Grandma Caroline, for all the times you said, "Good girl," for introducing me to musical theater, and for acknowledging my soul and heart.

Thank you to all my spiritual mentors on the path to self-discovery, especially Dr. James Mellon, who challenged me to confront my shadows and step into the light.

Thank you to Terry Sheehan, a lifelong friend and my past-life therapist, for all those days when we wondered what "normal people" do on Saturday afternoons. Thanks for traveling time and space with me.

Thank you to Lori Savage, who created the beautifully magical cover that holds my written thoughts within these pages.

Thank you to Thor Challgren, whose expertise helped me bring this book into print.

Thank you to my proofreader, Sue Buckley, who encouraged me to find new words to describe old feelings and for dotting my i's and crossing my t's.

Thank you to my children. I am deeply grateful for the gift of motherhood which allowed me to grow alongside them. I honor their uniqueness, kindness, and strength as human beings during this challenging time in history.

Thank you to my grandchildren who are intuitive, resilient, open, and strong. I believe they, along with their generation, embody the spirit of evolution necessary for our species.

To my "was-band" and to all my past lovers: Thank you for playing your roles in the unfolding of my life and growth, both by my casting and your own.

Thank you to women everywhere who have traveled the road of oppression and rebirth.

Thank you for the courage to fall and rise again. Thank you for being role models for me. Your resilience, despite the constant attempts to diminish your power, is inspiring. It is our time, and the world will be better for it. Love, joy, and peace are our destiny!

www.ingramcontent.com/pod-product-compliance
Lightning Source LLC
Chambersburg PA
CBHW030824090426
42737CB00009B/863